BREACH OF TRUST

Physician Participation in Executions in the United States

The American College of Physicians
Human Rights Watch
The National Coalition to Abolish the Death Penalty
Physicians for Human Rights

Library of Congress Catalog Card No.: 93-81272
ISBN 1-56432-125-8

Copies of this report may be obtained by contacting any of the following organizations:

THE AMERICAN COLLEGE OF PHYSICIANS

The American College of Physicians (ACP) is a non-profit, professional association of physicians trained in internal medicine — the nonsurgical diagnosis and treatment of disease in adults. The College was founded in 1915 to uphold high standards in medical ethics, education, research and practice, with the overarching goal of ensuring the quality of patient care. It is the nation's largest medical specialty society, with a membership of more than 80,000 internists, including primary care physicians, subspecialists, medical researchers and educators, and physicians-in-training.

The ACP publishes its code of ethics in the *Ethics Manual*, now in its third edition. In each edition, the ACP has been resolute in its opposition to physician participation in executions. The College has taken no position on the death penalty itself, considering it a matter of personal moral conscience. However, the ACP considers physician participation in the execution of prisoners to be unethical and contrary to the mission of the medical profession.

Members of the 1993-1994 Ethics Committee include: Christine K. Cassel, M.D., chair; Troyen A. Brennan, M.D., Richard J. Carroll, M.D.; Errol D. Crook, M.D.; Lee Dunn, Jr., Esq.; Lloyd W. Kitchens, M.D.; Capt. John Mitas, M.D.; and Susan W. Tolle, M.D.

Address for The American College of Physicians
Independence Mall West
Sixth Street at Race
Philadelphia, PA 19016-1572
Tel: (215) 351-2400
Fax: (215) 351-2869

HUMAN RIGHTS WATCH

Human Rights Watch conducts regular, systematic investigations of human rights abuses in some seventy countries around the world. It addresses the human rights practices of governments of all political stripes, of all geopolitical alignments, and of all ethnic and religious persuasions. In internal wars it documents violations by both governments and rebel groups. Human Rights Watch defends freedom of thought and expression, due process and equal protection of the law; it documents and denounces murders, disappearances, torture, arbitrary imprisonment, exile, censorship and other abuses of internationally recognized human rights.

Human Rights Watch began in 1978 with the founding of its Helsinki division. Today, it includes five divisions covering Africa, the Americas, Asia, the Middle East, as well as the signatories of the Helsinki accords. It also includes four collaborative projects on arms, free expression, prison conditions, and women's rights. It maintains offices in New York, Washington, Los Angeles, London, Moscow, Belgrade, Zagreb and Hong Kong. Human Rights Watch is an independent, nongovernmental organization, supported by contributions from private individuals and foundations. It accepts no government funds, directly or indirectly.

The staff includes Kenneth Roth, executive director; Cynthia Brown, program director; Holly J. Burkhalter, advocacy director; Allyson Collins, research associate; Richard Dicker, associate counsel; Jamie Fellner, planning coordinator; Ham Fish, senior advisor; Barbara Guglielmo, comptroller; Robert Kimzey, publications director; Gara LaMarche, associate director; Michal Longfelder, development director; Ellen Lutz, California director; Juan Méndez, general counsel; Susan Osnos, communications director; Dinah PoKempner, research associate; Jemera Rone, counsel; Rachel Weintraub, special events director; and Derrick Wong, finance and administration director.

The regional directors of Human Rights Watch are Abdullahi An-Na'im, Africa; Juan E. Méndez, Americas; Sidney Jones, Asia; Jeri Laber, Helsinki; and Andrew Whitley, Middle East. The project directors are Kenneth Anderson, Arms Project; Gara LaMarche, Free Expression Project; Joanna Weschler, Prison Project; and Dorothy Q. Thomas, Women's Rights Project.

The board includes Robert L. Bernstein, chair; Adrian W. DeWind, vice chair; Roland Algrant, Lisa Anderson, Peter D. Bell, Alice L. Brown, William Carmichael, Dorothy Cullman, Irene Diamond, Jonathan Fanton, Alan Finberg, Jack Greenberg, Alice H. Henkin, Stephen L. Kass, Marina Pinto Kaufman, Alexander MacGregor, Peter Osnos, Kathleen Peratis, Bruce Rabb, Orville Schell, Gary G. Sick, and Malcolm Smith.

Addresses for Human Rights Watch

485 Fifth Avenue
New York, NY 10017-6104
Tel: (212) 972-8400
Fax: (212) 972-0905
email: hrwatchnyc@igc.apc.org

10951 West Pico Blvd., #203
Los Angeles, CA 90064
Tel: (310) 475-3070
Fax: (310) 475-5613
email: hrwatchla@igc.apc.org

1522 K Street, N.W., #910
Washington, DC 20005
Tel: (202) 371-6592
Fax: (202) 371-0124
email: hrwatchdc@igc.apc.org

90 Borough High Street
London, UK SE1 1LL
Tel: (071) 378-8008
Fax: (071) 378-8029
email: hrwatchuk@gn.apc.org

THE NATIONAL COALITION TO ABOLISH
THE DEATH PENALTY

When the U.S. Supreme Court overturned the nation's death penalty laws in 1972, the committed activists who had been fighting for years to end executions thought their work was done. But in 1976, the Court re-opened the way for executions by accepting as constitutional, new death penalty statutes supposedly designed to eliminate the arbitrary and racist imposition of death sentences to which the Court had objected. As life once again came to the nation's death rows, the American Civil Liberties Union initiated the creation of The National Coalition to Abolish the Death Penalty (NCADP) in 1976.

The National Coalition to Abolish the Death Penalty (NCADP) leads and coordinates the movement to end state killing in the United States. Its 120 member organizations include civil and human rights groups, legal advocacy and public interest groups, and virtually every major church or religious denomination in the country. Although each constituent group has its own reasons for opposing capital punishment, all agree that justice and public safety require ending executions.

The Coalition believes that abolition will come from a multi-faceted approach : the general public must be constantly educated about the problems inherent in the death penalty; churches must continually challenge the morality of executions; Courts must hear challenges to its constitutionality; and the issue must remain a focus of the national debate on violence, crime, and how we respond to them. The NCADP works to facilitate and coordinate in each of these areas.

As the only national level organization working solely on abolition, the NCADP serves as a resource clearinghouse, and as an organizing and support center for nationwide efforts to end the death penalty.

The board of directors includes Sister Helen Prejean, Chair; Hugo Bedau, Vice-Chair; Pat Clark, Vice-Chair; Marshall Dayan, Vice-Chair; Linda Thurston, Vice-Chair; Kathy Lancaster, Secretary; Beth Ansheles, Treasurer. At-large members are Therese Bangert; Lillie Clark; Mike Farrell; Jonathan Gradess; Ron Hampton; Jane Henderson; Brenda Lewis; Freddie Nixon; Kathy Norgard; Henry Schwarzschild; Hilary Shelton; Sam Reese Sheppard; Earl Shinholster; Jim Sunderland.

Ashanti Chimurenga, Kica Matos, Diann Rust-Tierney, National Strategy Committee chairs; Lisa Radelet, Conference Committee chair; Earl Bonder, Development Committee chair; Cathy Ansheles, Membership Committee chair; Pat Bane, Murder Victim's Families chair; Jane Motz, Personnel Committee chair; Bob Domer, Religious Community Committee chair.

The staff includes Leigh Dingerson, executive director; Robert Gross, associate director; Pamela Rutter, program coordinator; Gerri Traina, development coordinator; Ricardo Villalobos, organizing coordinator; Flo Achtnich and Kurt Rosenberg are volunteers; Sandra Hinson, Bill Wu, and Dan Gritti are interns.

Address for The National Coalition to Abolish the Death Penalty
1325 G Street, NW LL-B
Washington, DC 20005
Tel: (202) 347-2411
Fax: (202) 347-2510

PHYSICIANS FOR HUMAN RIGHTS

Physicians for Human Rights (PHR) is an organization of physicians and other health professionals that brings the knowledge and skills of the medical sciences to the investigation and prevention of violations of international human rights and humanitarian law. PHR works to apply the special skills of health professionals to stop torture, "disappearances" and political killings by governments and opposition groups; to report on conditions and protection of detainees in prisons and refugee camps; to investigate the physical and psychological consequences of violations of humanitarian law and medical ethics in internal and international conflicts; to defend the right of civilians and combatants to receive medical care during times of war; to protect health professionals who are victims of human rights abuses; and to prevent medical complicity in torture and other human rights abuses.

Since 1986, PHR has sent over 40 fact-finding and emergency missions to over 25 countries. PHR bases its actions on the Universal Declaration of Human Rights and other international human rights and humanitarian agreements. The organization adheres to a policy of strict impartiality and is concerned with the medical consequences of human rights abuses regardless of the ideology of the offending government or group.

H. Jack Geiger, M.D. is President; Carola Eisenberg, M.D. is Vice President. The Board of Directors includes: Holly G. Atkinson, M.D.; Hon. J. Kenneth Blackwell; Kevin Cahill, M.D.; Charles Clements, M.D.; John Constable, M.D.; Robert Cook-Deegan, M.D.; Paul Epstein, M.D. ; Robert Kirchner, M.D.; Jennifer Learning, M.D.; Aryeh Neier; Jane Green Schaller, M.D.; M. Roy Schwarz, M.D.; Kim Thorburn, M.D.; Philippe Villers, M.D.

The staff includes: Eric Stover, executive director; Susannah Sirkin, deputy director; Kari Hannibal, membership and education coordinator; Gina VanderLoop, development director; Barbara Ayotte, senior program associate; Shana Swiss, M.D., director of Women's Program; Vincent Iacopino, M.D., Western Regional Representative; and Clyde C. Snow, senior forensic consultant.

Address for Physicians for Human Rights
100 Boylston Street
Suite 702
Boston, MA 02116
Tel: (617) 695-0041
Fax: (617) 695-0307
email: phrusa@igc.apc.org

CONTENTS

ACKNOWLEDGMENTS

This project was coordinated by Ellen Marshall, Policy Coordinator of the American College of Physicians (ACP); Joanna Weschler, Director of the Prison Project and Gara LaMarche, Associate Director of Human Rights Watch (HRW); Leigh Dingerson, Executive Director of the National Coalition to Abolish the Death Penalty (NCADP); and Susannah Sirkin, Deputy Director of Physicians for Human Rights (PHR). All contributed to the research, writing and editing of the report.

Janet Weiner, M.P.H., Research Associate of the ACP, was the principal writer and editor.

Kim Thorburn, M.D., of the ACP Human Rights and Medical Practice Subcommittee and the PHR Board of Directors, provided invaluable advice, editorial comment and coordinated interviews of prison doctors. Ron Shansky, M.D., M.P.H, Steve Spencer, M.D., and Armond Start, M.D., M.P.H., conducted formal interviews with prison doctors. NCADP interns Sandra Hinson, Bill Wu and Dan Gritti assisted with statute research and interviews of witnesses. Lamia Matta, then associate with the Human Rights Watch Prison Project, and Michael Hintze, intern with Human Rights Watch, assisted in research on state statutes and regulations.

Gregg Bloche, M.D., J.D., Associate Professor of Law, Georgetown University and consultant to PHR, was the principal researcher and writer for the section on medical ethics. Troyen Brennan, M.D., J.D., M.P.H., Professor of Law and Public Health, Harvard School of Public Health, also contributed to this section.

Henry Schwarzschild, member of the NCADP Executive Board, provided invaluable advice and assisted with statute research. Jim Welsh, Medical Advisor at Amnesty International, contributed historical references and a wealth of knowledge and analysis. David Rothman, Ph.D., Director of the Center for the Study of Society and Medicine, Columbia University College of Physicians and Surgeons, provided advice on and edited the section on ethics.

Lee Tucker, W. Bradford Wiley Fellow with Human Rights Watch, helped with fact checking. Anthony Levintow and Lydda Ragasa, HRW Associates, and Barbara Ayotte, PHR Program Associate provided valuable production assistance.

The participants in the project also express appreciation to Quentin D. Young, M.D., immediate-past Chair, ACP Human Rights and Medical Practice Subcommittee, Dr. Christine Cassel, M.D., Chair, ACP Human Rights and Medical Practice Subcommittee and ACP Ethics Committee, and Linda Johnson White, Director, ACP, Department of Scientific Policy, for their support in the development of this report and their continuing leadership in addressing physician participation in executions.

FOREWORD

Physicians as a group, hold a valued and sensitive position in society. We are granted the privilege of practicing medicine with the understanding that we will use our knowledge and skills in the public interest, and in each patient's best interests. This is a responsibility we take very seriously.

Physician participation in capital punishment poses a direct threat to the ethics of our profession. The American Medical Association's (AMA) ethical opinion on this issue is very clear and has not wavered over time. It is inappropriate for society to ask physicians, as members of a profession dedicated to healing and comfort of the sick, to participate in capital punishment. Our position is as follows:

> An individual's opinion on capital punishment is the personal moral decision of the individual. A physician, as a member of a profession dedicated to preserving life when there is hope of doing so, should not be a participant in a legally authorized execution.
>
> —*1992 Code of Medical Ethics, Current Opinions of the Council on Ethical and Judicial Affairs of the American Medical Association (article 2.06)*

Furthermore, where state laws or regulations require involvement, the AMA recommends that state medical societies work through the legislative process to change the pertinent criminal codes, and that the societies inform state licensure boards and certification and recertification agencies.

This report documents the extent of physician participation in law, regulation and practice. It vividly portrays the conflicts that arise when medical skills are used to facilitate executions. As such, it should serve as a valuable resource for physicians, legislators, and correctional officials in efforts to ensure that professional ethics are upheld in all social and legal contexts.

M. Roy Schwarz, M.D.
Senior Vice-President, Medical Education and Science
American Medical Association

1
INTRODUCTION

When Charles Walker was executed by lethal injection in Illinois on September 12, 1990, three physicians assisted. Their medical skills were used to establish the intravenous portal through which the lethal preparation would pass, to witness and monitor the execution procedure and, in the end, to pronounce death. This occurred despite the appeals from many medical organizations to then Governor James Thompson urging that the state not use physicians to implement the execution. A few months following the execution, the Illinois legislature passed a bill providing for the anonymity of all persons participating in Illinois executions. Again, despite protest from the medical profession, Illinois' new governor, James Edgar, signed the bill into law.

The Walker execution and the action of the Illinois legislature brought the issue of physician participation in executions to the attention of many medical professionals and groups. These events brought into sharp focus the discrepancy between medical ethics and state laws on this subject. The ongoing controversy prompted a number of organizations to join together to examine the extent of physician involvement in executions and to provide policy recommendations to medical organizations, state governments and departments of corrections.

Four organizations participated in this project: the American College of Physicians (ACP), Physicians for Human Rights (PHR), Human Rights Watch (HRW) and the National Coalition to Abolish the Death Penalty (NCADP). As the working group began its project, members agreed on the nature and focus of its work. Each organization has different viewpoints on the death penalty itself, and all members agreed that this report would not take a position supporting or opposing capital punishment. Instead, the project would focus on medical involvement in executions, and the need to explore and define the ethical boundaries of such conduct.[1] We also decided to narrow the scope of the project to

---

[1] The American College of Physicians and Physicians for Human Rights have not taken a position on capital punishment, but oppose physician involvement on ethical and human rights grounds; Human Rights Watch and the National Coalition to Abolish the Death Penalty are opposed to capital punishment in all

1

physician involvement only, although we would point out when other health professionals participated in executions. Finally, we agreed to focus on execution procedures, rather than on related issues, such as physicians' role in sentencing or conducting autopsies.

Early in the project, the group realized the need for accurate data upon which to base policy recommendations. The extent of physician participation in executions, especially since the death penalty was reinstated by the U.S. Supreme Court in 1976, was not well documented. Therefore, we undertook research to systematically compile the necessary information, asking the following questions:

- What are the requirements in state statutes and regulations regarding physician participation in executions?
- What is the actual practice, prevalence and nature of physician participation in the execution process?
- Are provisions made for medical staff to refuse involvement without reprisal? Are there procedures for raising and investigating ethical violations?
- What are the policies of state and national medical societies regarding the ethical standards of physician involvement in executions, and what disciplinary procedures are in place in cases of violations of those standards?

We reviewed all state laws (which are in the public record); we requested regulations (which are not always a matter of public record) from each state's department of corrections. All state medical associations were surveyed for their policies regarding physician participation in executions. Finally, interviews with witnesses and physicians were conducted to obtain case reports of actual participation in executions.

The results of this research form the basis of the following report. We begin in Chapter 2 with a short introduction to the history of physician participation in executions. We follow that in Chapter 3 with a review of medical organizations' responses to the issue . A summary of the results of our research appears in Chapter 4 (with a state-by-state description of laws, regulations and professional policies in the Appendix). Chapter 5 sets out the ethical framework for the prohibition against physician participation in the death penalty, and points out areas of

---

circumstances.

consensus and controversy. Finally, our policy recommendations appear in Chapter 6.

This report documents that physicians continue to be involved in executions, in violation of ethical and professional codes of conduct. This involvement is often mandated by state law and specified in departmental regulations about execution procedures. Even when state laws are vague about requiring physician participation, our research indicates that in practice, physicians are often directly involved in the execution process. As more states attempt to create the appearance of humane, sterile or painless executions, lawmakers and corrections officials may look to physicians to apply their medical skills for this purpose. But execution is not a medical procedure, and is not within the scope of medical practice. Physicians are committed to humanity and the relief of suffering; they are entrusted by society to work for the benefit of their patients and the public. This trust is shattered when medical skills are used to facilitate state executions.

Our recommendations are designed to ensure that current U.S. laws do not require physicians to violate professional ethics. Society must decide whether, how and when to impose capital punishment--without involving physicians in the execution process.

METHOD OF EXECUTION: ELECTROCUTION

METHOD OF EXECUTION: HANGING

METHOD OF EXECUTION: LETHAL GAS

METHOD OF EXECUTION: FIRING SQUAD

METHOD OF EXECUTION: LETHAL INJECTION

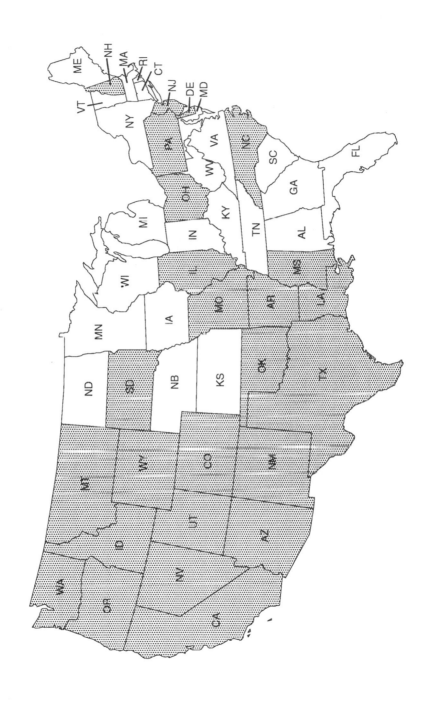

METHODS OF EXECUTION: BY STATE

TABLE 1

State	Lethal Injection	Electro- cution	Lethal Gas	Hanging	Firing Squad
AL		X			
AZ	X		X		
AR	X	X			
CA	X		X		
CO	X				
CT		X			
DE	X			X	
FL		X			
GA		X			
ID	X				X
IN		X			
IL	X				
KY		X			
LA	X				
MD			X		
MS	X		X		
MO	X				
MT	X			X	
NB		X			
NV	X				
NH	X				
NJ	X				
NM	X				
NC	X		X		
OH	X	X			
OK	X				
OR	X				
PA	X				
SC		X			
SD	X				
TN		X			
TX	X				
UT	X				X
VA		X			
WA	X			X	
WY	X				

2
BACKGROUND

The United States is one of the few democracies that continues to impose and carry out the death penalty. In addition to the federal government and the U.S. military, 36 states have death penalty statutes. Methods of execution include lethal injection, electrocution, the gas chamber, hanging, and the firing squad. Twenty-five states have designated lethal injection as either the mandatory or an optional method of execution; the United States is the only country in the world currently using this method. Electrocution remains in practice in 12 states, while the gas chamber is used in five states. Hangings can still be carried out in three states, and firing squads can be used in two states. [See TABLE 1 and maps of Methods of Execution: by State.] An examination of the history of the death penalty in the United States reveals that the relatively wide array of execution methods can be explained in part by constant efforts to find more "humane" avenues of execution.

EXECUTION METHODS

Influenced by English common law tradition, American colonies inflicted the death penalty on criminals by various methods, including being pressed to death, drawn and quartered, and burned at the stake.[2] After the ratification of the Eighth Amendment's ban on "cruel and unusual punishment" in 1789, hanging was considered the only constitutionally permissible method of execution for most of the next century. The one exception to this rule was the use of a firing squad in Utah, which was upheld by the Supreme Court in 1878.

In New York State botched public hangings in the mid-19th century provided the impetus for a more humane method of execution.[3] A state commission, chaired by a dentist, was formed to investigate alternative methods of executions. The advent of electricity in the late

---

[2] Bedau H. *The Death Penalty in America*. New York: Oxford University Press, 1982.

[3] Jones GR. Judicial electrocution and the prison doctor. *Lancet* 1990;713-714.

1880's introduced a new method of execution to the legal system. Thomas Edison himself testified that death by electrocution would be instantaneous.[4] After the commission recommended electrocution as the most humane method of execution, New York State approved the construction of an electric chair in 1888. In 1890, William Kemmler became the first prisoner to die in the electric chair. An eyewitness account described how 1400 volts for 17 seconds was insufficient, and how Kemmler began to recover a minute later. There was a delay of two minutes before a further shock lasting two and a half minutes was administered. Smoke rose from the burnt corpse.[5] An autopsy report showed that Kemmler's flesh had been severely burned at the points of contact with the electrodes.[6]

The electric chair was used to execute 695 men and women in New York over the next 75 years. Despite ongoing doubts about its efficiency and painlessness, electrocution quickly became the predominant method of execution in the country, with more than half of death penalty states using it by the end of the 1920's.

In 1921, Nevada became the first state to approve the use of lethal gas in executions. Discontent with the mixed results of electrocution, the legislature approved release of lethal gas into a condemned prisoner's cell, while he or she was asleep. Gassing was never used as originally envisioned: for practical purposes, it could not be carried out in prisoners' cells; a special chamber had to be built. In 1924 in Nevada, Gee Jon became the first person to be executed in a gas chamber. Seven other states adopted the gas chamber by the end of the 1930's. By 1960, three more states had chosen the gas chamber as the preferred method of execution.

A Supreme Court decision in 1972 extended a de facto moratorium in executions that began in 1967. The decision forced states to review and revise their capital punishment laws. At that point, a total of 5,500 people had been executed since the beginning of the century. In *Furman* v. *Georgia*, the Court invalidated the Georgia system because

---

[4] Beichmann A. The first electrocution. *Commentary* 1963; 35:410-419.

[5] Jones GR. Judicial electrocution and the prison doctor. *Lancet* 1990;713-714.

[6] Beichmann A. The first electrocution. *Commentary* 1963; 35:410-419.

"the Eighth and Fourteenth Amendment cannot tolerate the infliction of a sentence of death under legal systems so wantonly and freakishly imposed."[7] Within the majority opinion, three justices affirmed the constitutionality of the death penalty, while two others came to the conclusion that its imposition under any circumstances would violate the "cruel and unusual punishment" clause of the Eighth Amendment.

The death penalty was reinstated in 1976, in a series of Supreme Court decisions.[8] These cases upheld the constitutionality of the death penalty in states that considered mitigating circumstances at the sentencing stage. The following year, Gary Gilmore was executed by firing squad in Utah. Public outcry over the use of a firing squad generated support for a new method of execution: lethal injection. In 1977, Oklahoma became the first state to approve use of lethal injection, with three other states quickly following suit. The first execution by lethal injection, that of Charles Brooks, took place in Texas in 1982.

PHYSICIAN INVOLVEMENT IN EXECUTIONS

Although lethal injection has brought renewed attention to the issue of medical participation in executions, doctors have played a role in carrying out the death penalty for many years. For example, during the French Revolution, Dr. Joseph Guillotin successfully promoted a head cutting device for executions, in the belief that the method was less painful than others being used. However, Dr. Guillotin was said to be scandalized by the name given the machine and the uses to which it was put.[9] The device was later perfected by a French surgeon, Dr. Antoine Louis, who redesigned the blade to make a cleaner cut.[10] In the United States, two physicians, Dr. Carlos MacDonald and Dr. E.C. Spitzka,

---

[7] *Furman* v. *Georgia*, 408 U.S. 238 (1972), Justice White, concurring.

[8] *Gregg* v. *Georgia*, 428 U.S. 153; *Proffitt* v. *Florida*, 428 U.S. 242; *Jurek* v. *Texas*, 428 U.S. 262.

[9] Donegan CF. Dr. Guillotin - reformer and humanitarian. *Journal of the Royal Society of Medicine* 1990;83:637-639.

[10] *Ibid*.

supervised the first execution by the electric chair. Their advice was crucial to the execution. In his autobiography, Dr. MacDonald wrote: "Before Kemmler was brought into the room, the warden asked the physicians how long the contact should be maintained. [I] replied, 'Twenty seconds...'"[11] According to news reports, Dr. Spitzka ordered the electric current to be turned off prematurely, after 17 seconds. When he discovered that Kemmler was still alive, Dr. Spitzka shouted, "Turn on the current instantly. This man is not dead."[12]

In 1980, a year before the first scheduled execution by lethal injection (of Thomas Hayes in Oklahoma), the American Medical Association (AMA) passed a resolution against physician participation in executions.   The resolution did not clearly define the actions that constitute "participation". Hayes' execution never took place, because his sentence was commuted. But in 1982, physicians played a prominent role in the first execution by lethal injection, that of Charles Brooks. News reports indicate that Dr. Ralph Gray, Medical Director of the Texas Department of Corrections, examined Mr. Brooks "to make certain his veins would accept lethal doses of drugs."[13] Describing the execution itself, the *London Guardian* reported:

> "After five minutes...Dr. Ralph Gray listened to his heart through a stethoscope, shook his head, and commented 'A couple more minutes'. Dr. Bascom Bentley, also checking the prisoner, flashed a torch into his eyes and asked the executioner: 'Is the injection completed?' He was told it was not. Two minutes later, after a further stethoscopic examination Dr. Gray said: 'I pronounce this man dead'."

Since that time, other physicians have participated in lethal injections, as well as in executions by other methods. In 1990, three physicians administered the first lethal injection execution in Illinois to Charles Walker. A judicial grant of anonymity kept their names

---

[11] Trombley S. *The Execution Protocol*, Crown Books: New York, 1992.

[12] Beichmann A. The first electrocution. *Commentary* 1963; 35:410-419.

[13] Reuters News Agency, December 9, 1992.

confidential. In Arkansas in 1992, the execution of Ricky Ray Rector was delayed for 45 minutes as the medical team attempted to find the vein in which to insert the catheter. At the time they were successful, the team was already preparing to surgically insert the intravenous tube.[14]

Physicians remain involved in other methods of executions as well. In Washington, Westley Allan Dodd was executed by hanging in January 1993. Dr. Donald Reay, King County Medical Examiner, reviewed the Washington State Penitentiary's preparations for the hanging and offered opinions on "the efficiency of the hanging procedures"* including cause and timing of death and the likelihood of pain. Dr. Reay has indicated that he is personally opposed to the death penalty and that the opinions he expressed "are based solely on present day medical evidence". (* sworn affidavit by Dr. Reay, July 16, 1992)

The law and medical ethics have begun to clash visibly around the issue of physician participation in executions. In 1991, Illinois passed a bill requiring the presence of at least two physicians in lethal injection executions and requiring that they pronounce death. The law shields the identity of the physicians by guaranteeing them anonymity, going so far as to stipulate that they can be paid in cash for their services. The bill was strongly opposed by the Chicago Medical Society, the Illinois State Medical Society, the AMA, the American College of Physicians (ACP), the American Public Health Association (APHA), the American Association for the Advancement of Science, the Institute of Medicine, and Physicians for Human Rights (PHR). Following this professional outcry, in 1992 Illinois amended the law to remove the mandated witnessing role for physicians, but kept intact the provisions about pronouncing death and anonymity.

The debate reached the federal level in 1992 when the U.S. Justice Department proposed new rules for federal executions. The last federal execution was conducted in 1963. Existing regulations require that the execution take place according to the criminal code of the state in which the federal prison is located. The new rules proposed use of lethal injections, and mandated that at least one physician attend the

---

[14] British Medical Association. *Medicine Betrayed: The Participation of Doctors in Human Rights Abuses* (London: Zed Books, 1992) p. 129.

[15] *New York Times*, January 8, 1993.

[16] *Ibid.*

execution and pronounce death.[17]   Once again, medical professionals
vigorously opposed the rule.   The AMA, ACP, the American Nurses
Association, the APHA, the Society for Correctional Physicians, and the
National Commission on Correctional Health Care all submitted written
comments on the proposal.   As a result, in early 1993 the Justice
Department eliminated the requirement that a physician be present and
that physicians be required to pronounce death.   However, the Justice
Department did not prohibit physician participation in executions.   As
then Attorney General William Barr stated in the Federal Register,
"Because the department may conclude that a physician's presence is
necessary to a responsible execution, physician participation will not be
barred.   However, [the regulation] has been revised to make clear that
medical professionals may decline to participate in executions on the basis
of national ethics."[18]

---

[17]   Department of Justice.   Implementation of death sentences in federal
cases.   Federal Register 1992; 57(230):56536.

[18]   Department of Justice.   Implementation of death sentences in federal
cases.   Federal Register 1993; 58(11):4690.

3
MEDICAL RESPONSES TO PHYSICIAN PARTICIPATION IN EXECUTIONS

The advent of lethal injections has prompted the medical community in the United States to clarify its position on physician involvement in executions, and to solidify its opposition to physician participation. By 1980, four states had passed lethal injection statutes. The same year, a landmark article in the *New England Journal of Medicine* detailed the history of medical participation in executions and ethical considerations. The authors concluded that lethal injection, by requiring medical knowledge and skills, was "a corruption and exploitation of the healing profession's role in society."[19] Later that year, the AMA Council on Ethical and Judicial Affairs issued a report that prohibited the participation of physicians in executions. The Council wrote:

> "An individual's opinion on capital punishment is the personal moral decision of the individual. A physician, as a member of a profession dedicated to preserving life when there is hope of doing so, should not be a participant in a legally authorized execution. A physician may make a determination or certification of death as currently provided by law in any situation."[20]

Other medical organizations followed suit. In 1981, the World Medical Association (WMA) stated that it was unethical for physicians to participate in executions, except to certify death.[21] In a press release, the Secretary General of the WMA said:

---

[19] Curran WJ, Casscells W. The ethics of medical participation in capital punishment. *New England Journal of Medicine* 1980;302:226-230.

[20] Opinion 2.06 of the Council on Ethical and Judicial Affairs of the American Medical Association: Capital Punishment. In: *1992 Code of Ethics: Annotated Current Opinions.* Chicago, IL: American Medical Association, 1992.

[21] World Medical Association, Resolution on physician participation in capital punishment, September 1981.

"Acting as an executioner is not the practice of medicine and physician services are not required to carry out capital punishment even if the methodology utilizes pharmacologic agents or equipment that might otherwise be used in the practice of medicine."[22]

Similar pronouncements were made by the American College of Physicians in 1984, and the American Public Health Association (APHA) in 1985.[23] The APHA resolution applied to other health professionals as well, stating that "health personnel, as members of a profession dedicated to preserving life when there is hope of doing so, should not be required or expected to assist in legally authorized executions."[24] Other health professional organizations also took notice of participation in executions. The American Nurses Association in 1983 declared that participation was a breach of the ethical tradition of nursing.[25]

The Walker execution in Illinois in 1990, and the shield of anonymity around the participating physicians, catalyzed further action on the issue by organized medicine. In 1991, the ACP sponsored a resolution to the AMA requesting that the Council on Ethical and Judicial Affairs develop a guideline clearly defining physician participation in executions. The following year, the Council reaffirmed its 1980 position, and clarified the AMA prohibition on participation.

The Council report clarified the distinction between determining and certifying death. "Determining death includes monitoring the condition of the condemned during the execution and determining the

---

[22] *Ibid.*

[23] American College of Physicians Ethics Manual. *Annals of Internal Medicine* 1984; 101:263-74. American Public Health Association. Position Paper 8521: Participation of Health Professionals in Capital Punishment. In: APHA Public Policy Statements 1948-present, cumulative. Washington, DC: APHA, 1993.

[24] American Public Health Association. Position Paper 8521: Participation of Health Professionals in Capital Punishment. In: APHA Public Policy Statements 1948-present, cumulative. Washington, DC: APHA, 1993.

[25] American Nurses Association. *Code for Nurses with Interpretive Statements.* Kansas City: ANA, 1983.

point at which the individual has actually died. Certifying death includes confirming that the individual is dead after another person has pronounced or determined that the individual is dead."[26] The Council defined participation to include:

- prescribing or administering tranquilizers and other psychotropic agents and medications that are part of the execution procedure;

- monitoring vital signs on site or remotely (including monitoring electrocardiograms);

- attending or observing an execution as a physician;

- rendering of technical advice regarding execution.

And in the case of lethal injection, the guidelines specify that physician participation includes:

- selecting injection sites;

- starting intravenous lines as a port for a lethal injection device;

- prescribing, preparing, administering, or supervising injection drugs or their doses or types;

- inspecting, testing, or maintaining lethal injection devices;

- consulting with or supervising lethal injection personnel.

The guidelines also specified actions that do *not* constitute physician participation in executions:

- testifying as to the competence to stand trial, testifying as to relevant medical evidence during trial, or testifying as to medical

---

[26] Council on Ethical and Judicial Affairs. Physician participation in capital punishment. *Journal of the American Medical Association* 1993;270:365-368.

aspects of aggravating or mitigating circumstances during the
penalty phase of a capital case;

- certifying death, provided that the condemned has been declared
  dead by another person;

- witnessing an execution in a totally nonprofessional capacity;

- witnessing an execution at the specific voluntary request of the
  condemned person, provided that the physician observes the
  execution in a non-physician capacity and takes no action that
  would constitute physician participation in an execution;

- relieving the acute suffering of a condemned person while
  awaiting execution, including providing tranquilizers at the
  specific voluntary request of the condemned person to help
  relieve pain or anxiety in anticipation of the execution.

The Council chose not to issue guidelines on psychiatric
involvement in executions, including evaluation of an inmate's
competence to be executed, and treatment to restore an inmate's
competence to be executed. The Council decided to consult further with
the American Psychiatric Association before issuing such guidelines. It is
expected that the Council will consider the issue in 1994. In Chapter 5
of this report, we explore the ethics of psychiatric participation and
suggest reasonable guidelines.

The Council guidelines are clear about which medical activities
constitute physician participation in executions. In the next chapter, we
highlight the conflicts between these ethical guidelines and the role
prescribed for physicians in state law and correctional department
regulations about executions.

4
RESULTS OF THE STUDY: PHYSICIAN PARTICIPATION — IN LAW, REGULATION AND PRACTICE

The relevant statutes of the thirty-six states with the death penalty mention the presence of a physician in all but two cases. Some statutes appear to be in direct conflict with AMA ethical standards, based on the newly adopted report. Twenty-three states require that a physician "determine" or "pronounce" death. Twenty-eight state statutes or regulations require that a physician "shall" or "must" be present at the execution. Other statutes simply list a physician among the witnesses. The language of the statutes is sometimes vague, and curiously awkward. In several states the warden or superintendent "shall invite" a physician to attend. In Utah the director "shall cause a physician to attend" the execution.

The language in statutes about lethal injection clearly expresses a desire to set it apart from other medical procedures. Currently, twenty-five states use lethal injection (fourteen as the sole method and eleven as an option). Eleven of these statutes declare outright that lethal injection is not a medical procedure. Seven also authorize pharmacists to dispense lethal drugs to the Commissioner (or designee) without a prescription.

Within each state, the department of corrections usually designs its own set of regulations, often detailed, for conducting executions. They translate the usually vague language of the statute into specific assignments for physicians involved in executions. Unlike state laws, which are always matters of public record, these regulations are frequently difficult to obtain. In a few states, the documents are confidential under state law.

For the purposes of this report, we were able to obtain regulations directly from the departments of corrections in response to a written request from Human Rights Watch, or indirectly in the course of further research. In a few states, particularly those that have not conducted executions since 1976, departmental regulations regarding the process of execution do not exist. In the Appendix, we provide a state-by-state overview of the information available.

We found that nondescript statutes "inviting" a physician to an execution can translate into specific procedures directing physician

involvement in executions. In Arizona, where the method of execution
is either the gas chamber or lethal injection, the law states that the
superintendent "shall invite" the presence of a physician. The regulations
specify that the Chief of Health Services shall "arrange for a physician to
be present during the execution of a condemned inmate to operate the
heart monitor."[27] Similarly, in California (which uses the gas chamber
or lethal injection) the law indicates only that two physicians must be
invited. But San Quentin regulations stipulate that on the day of
execution, the Chief Medical Officer will "attend with another staff
physician, and by monitoring the heart of the inmate, or by whatever
means appropriate, determine or pronounce death."[28] The regulations
go on to delineate that one of the attending physicians must direct the
fitting of a heart monitor to the condemned inmate approximately 15
minutes before execution, and that the heart monitor must be activated
five minutes before the execution. The physician must also advise the
warden that the prisoner has died.

In Oklahoma, a lethal injection state, the law indicates that the
presence of a physician must be "invited". But Oklahoma Department of
Corrections procedures stipulate that the physician must inspect the
catheter and monitoring equipment and determine that the fluid will flow
into the inmate's vein.[29] The procedures also specify that the
Department of Corrections' Medical Director must order a sufficient
quantity of the substances used in the execution.

Oregon law, which mandates lethal injections, also states that a
physician's presence must be invited. But departmental procedures
specify that the physician "will be responsible for observing the execution
process and examining the condemned after the lethal substance(s) has

---

[27] Arizona State Prison Complex-Florence Internal Management Procedure
500 - Execution Procedures: §5.5.3.

[28] San Quentin Institutional Procedures, §VI.A.9.c.

[29] Department of Corrections Policy Statement No. OP-090901: "Procedures
for the Execution of Inmates Sentenced to Death." Cited in: *Medicine Betrayed: The
Participation of Doctors in Human Rights Abuses*, 1992, p. 112.

been administered to ensure that death is induced."[30]   Oregon regulations also stipulate that a "medically trained individual" administer the lethal injection. This has implications for other health professionals, many of whom are also bound by ethical codes that prohibit participation in executions. The Oregon regulations state:

> "A medically trained individual as designated by the health services manager will insert a catheter into an appropriate vein and cause an infusion of normal saline...The medically trained individual...will by syringe first introduce a lethal barbiturate, then open the drip regulator...then introduce the chemical paralytic agents into the inmate. The intravenous administration of the chemicals will be maintained until death is pronounced by the licensed physician(s)."

In Florida, where the method of execution is electrocution, the law stipulates that a physician shall be present to announce "when death has been inflicted." However, Florida prison regulations specify that a physician and physician's assistant are to be among the five people in the execution chamber immediately prior to and throughout the execution.[31] The regulations also state that the Chief Medical Officer of the prison is responsible for procuring two physicians and a medical technician for the execution. Two minutes after the electrical current ceases, one of the physicians must examine the body for vital signs and pronounce the inmate dead.

In North Carolina, where lethal injections and gas chamber executions are allowed, the law states that a surgeon or physician from a penitentiary must be one of the witnesses. The Department of Corrections' Research File provides further details:

> "When lethal injection is used, the inmate is secured with lined ankle and wrist restraints to a gurney in the

---

[30]   Oregon Department of Corrections Rule #24 (Tab 66), Capital Punishment, Death by Lethal Injection. OAR 291-24-045.

[31] Florida State Prison Operating Procedure.

preparation room outside the chamber. Two saline intravenous lines are started, one in each arm...appropriately trained personnel then enter behind the curtain and connect the cardiac monitor leads, the injection devices and the stethoscope to the appropriate leads...thiopental sodium is injected which puts the inmate into a deep sleep. A second chemical agent, procuronium bromide, follows. This agent is a total muscle relaxer. The inmate stops breathing and dies soon afterward. A physician, whose sole function is to pronounce the inmate dead, watches from the control room. After five to ten minutes, he goes to the inmate, listens for heart sounds, and pronounces him dead."[32]

When the gas chamber is used in North Carolina, the regulations specify that the inmate be fitted with a heart monitor, which can be read by a physician and a staff member in the control room. After the physician pronounces the inmate dead, ammonia is pumped into the execution chamber to neutralize the gas.

New Jersey law states that two licensed physicians are "authorized to be present" at executions, which are accomplished by lethal injection. The Administrative Code specifies who these physicians should be, and what they should do.[33] The Medical Director of the Department of Corrections must be one of the physicians, while the other is selected from a list of volunteers from other correctional institutions. In the event that no volunteers are available, the Department must contract with physicians in the community. The code stipulates that the execution chamber be equipped with a cardiac monitor, which "shall be positioned to provide visual access to the team physicians." During the execution, the physicians view the condemned and the cardiac monitor, and upon completion of the procedures, "examine the deceased and confirm death." The New Jersey Code refers to the lethal chemicals as "execution medications".

---

[32] Department of Corrections Research File: Methods of Execution in North Carolina.

[33] New Jersey Administrative Code 10A:16 - 10.8-10.14.

As these examples illustrate, the regulations are much more specific than the statutes in describing the role of physicians in executions. Often when the statutes indicate that the physicians' presence is tentative, the regulations leave no doubt about their part in the process.

WHAT REALLY HAPPENS

But even regulations cannot reliably describe the events as they occur. To understand the full extent of physician involvement in executions, we conducted interviews with witnesses to recent executions. These anecdotes and other published statements indicate that current execution procedures require physicians to violate professional ethical standards. They also document the inherent problems in continuing attempts to define a "bright line" standard for the actions that constitute "participation".

As discussed in Chapter 3, the AMA guidelines clearly state that determining death, as opposed to certifying death, constitutes physician participation in execution. Determining death includes monitoring the condemned person and determining the point at which death occurs. Our research indicates that in practice, this guideline is often ignored.

Mississippi

According to a former warden, prison staff medical technicians attach two EKG monitors and two stethoscopes to the prisoner's chest in an isolation cell a few paces from the gas chamber. The medical technicians leave. After the inmate is brought to the gas chamber, the EKG and stethoscopes are monitored by two physicians, who sit behind the chamber out of view of the official witnesses. The physicians are local doctors who volunteer for the task and are not paid. They are not identified to the witnesses, and wear civilian clothes. Once the cyanide pellets are dropped, the doctors monitor the EKG and advise the warden when the prisoner has expired. The body is then examined by the County Coroner (not a physician) who has witnessed the execution. The doctor shows him the EKG, and the Coroner certifies death.[34]

---

[34] Interview with Donald Cabana, former warden at Parchman Prison in Mississippi. September 24, 1992.

Virginia

According to a criminologist who witnessed three executions, a physician (employed by the Department of Corrections) awaits completion of the execution in a small conference room directly off the execution chamber. After the electric chair is turned off, there is a three minute "cooling period". The doctor enters the chamber and places a stethoscope to the inmate's chest. The doctor pronounces that the inmate has expired.[35]

In the 1993 execution of Charles Stamper, a witness reported that the prison doctor wore a white lab coat as he put a stethoscope to Mr. Stamper's chest. Finding no heartbeat, the doctor said to the warden,"This man has expired."[36]

The AMA report anticipates the problem with the use of a physician to determine death. Inevitably, there will be instances where the physician finds that death has not occurred. In these cases, the physician must then signal to the executioner that the procedure must continue or recommence.

Alabama

In 1989, the execution of Horace Franklin Dunkins did not go as planned. One of the two doctors present recalled the procedure:

> "I was in the witness room adjacent to the execution chamber. I saw Dunkins in the electric chair and heard the generator start. At this time I did not see a strong contraction of Dunkins' muscles as had occurred at the two executions I had previously witnessed...
>
> After a short period of time, the other doctor... and I were called into the execution chamber. I could see that Dunkins was breathing. I was first into the chamber. Respirations were present and appeared normal. His muscles were clenched and his eyes were closed. I checked his peripheral pulse, in his wrist, and it was

---

[35] Interview with Robert Johnson, Chairman of the Department of Justice, Law and Society at American University, Washington, DC. September 11, 1992.

[36] *Richmond Time-Dispatch*, January 20, 1993.

normal. I listened to his heart and his heartbeat was strong with little irregularity...(the other doctor) checked Dunkins' level of consciousness with medically accepted tests for reaction to pain, a sternum rub and nipple pinch. Dunkins had no reaction to these tests.

I told an official that Dunkins was not dead. Dr. _____ and I then returned to the witness room. The blinds were closed but shortly thereafter opened again. I again heard the generator begin. This time, Dunkins' muscles contracted... Dr. _____ and I re-entered the chamber a few minutes later... Dunkins was not breathing. I examined him first and he had a weak heartbeat which rapidly diminished to no heartbeat. Dr. _____ and I each examined Dunkins twice on this second occasion. We agreed and reported that Dunkins was dead."[37]

Georgia

In 1984, electric current failed to kill Alpha Otis Stephens in the allotted time. As officials waited the required eight minutes for the body to cool before the body could be examined, witnesses watched as Stephens struggled to breathe, taking as many as 23 breaths. Two physicians examined him and reported that he was still alive. A second charge was administered, after which the two physicians re-examined Stephens and pronounced him dead.[38]

Indiana

The 1985 execution of William E. Vandiver also required multiple jolts. Dr. Rodger Saylors of Michigan City examined the body

---

[37]   Affidavit of John A. Vanlandingham, M.D., licensed to practice in Alabama. August 10, 1989.

[38]   *The New York Times*, December 13, 1984; *The St. Petersburg Evening Independent*, December 12, 1984.

and found that Vandiver was still alive. The current was applied three more times before Vandiver was pronounced dead.[39]

Other specific activities mentioned by the AMA that constitute unethical behavior by physicians include supervising or overseeing the preparation or administration of the execution process, and attending or observing the execution as a physician.

Mississippi

Two local physicians were called in to assist in three executions at Parchman Prison. In addition to monitoring heart activity during the executions, the doctors attended preparatory briefings with the execution team. One subject covered at the briefing was the procedure in the event of a malfunction of the gas chamber. In such a case, the execution team would look for a mechanical problem. The chamber would be cleared of gas, and the inmate removed to a holding cell. If the inmate was unconscious, one of the doctors was to remain with him until the chamber could be repaired. According to the procedure, the doctors would make a "medical judgment" as to whether to attempt to revive the prisoner.

The warden expressed relief that the problem did not occur in the three executions over which he presided.[40]

Lethal injection poses the most direct challenge to keeping physicians uninvolved in executions. The AMA guidelines recognize this and specify that selecting injection sites, starting intravenous lines, prescribing, preparing or administering injection drugs, and consulting with lethal injection personnel constitute physician participation in executions and are unethical.

Nevada

The Medical Director of the Nevada State Prison examines the prisoner during the week of the execution, to determine venous access. The Medical Director prescribes the three drugs used in the execution, which are obtained from a local hospital by the Department of

---

[39] *The New York Times*, October 17, 1985.

[40] Interview with Donald Cabana, former warden at Parchman Prison in Mississippi. September 24, 1992.

Corrections pharmacist. The pharmacist mixes and prepares the solution.[41]

The AMA Council report finds that some activities conducted by doctors do not constitute participation in executions. Yet our research indicates that in practice, even these activities raise questions in some circumstances. For example, the Council indicates that it is ethical for a physician to provide medical care to a condemned person if the individual gives informed consent, if the medical care is used to heal, comfort, or preserve the life of the condemned individual, and if the care does not facilitate the execution.

South Carolina

In 1991, Donald Gaskins attempted suicide about sixteen hours before his scheduled execution. Gaskins used a razor blade to slit his wrists and elbows. He passed out from loss of blood, and was found unconscious about an hour later. A physician was called in to treat Mr. Gaskins, and he stitched the inmates's wounds tightly, restricting movement of the arms. Gaskins remained unconscious, strapped down on a gurney in the cell. The doctor was in and out, periodically checking on his condition. He wrote extensive notes that he would not show to Gaskins' attorney.

One other doctor, a psychiatrist, was called in. They performed several exams for unconsciousness, the results of which are unknown. Just before the execution, Mr. Gaskins regained consciousness. He was escorted to the electric chair and executed.[42]

WHEN PHYSICIANS REFUSE

The issue of physician participation in executions poses special conflicts for physicians who work in correctional facilities. It dramatically highlights the tension that exists between correctional administrators and physicians who work in their institutions. Administrators may expect

---

[41] Interview with Mellonese Harrison, M.D., Senior Physician, Nevada State Prison. November 11, 1992.

[42] Telephone interview with Franklin W. Draper, attorney for Mr. Gaskins. August 7, 1992.

physicians to use medical skills to meet institutional needs, even for purposes other than the provision of health care. There are limited standards to guide physicians' responsibilities to an institution's wards (their patients) or to the employer institution. The lack of clarity about physicians' obligations causes inevitable conflicts between administrators and physicians.

It should be noted that the National Commission on Correctional Health Care (NCCHC) has standards for the accreditation of correctional health systems in the U.S. NCCHC standards prohibit the participation of correctional health professionals in all forms of punishment, which includes executions.[43] Unfortunately, accreditation is voluntary, and less than 15% of all state prison systems have gone through the NCCHC accreditation process.

Since many execution procedures call for medical skills, such as monitoring vital signs, cannulating veins and administering drugs, it is not hard to understand why administrators turn to institution-employed physicians for assistance. As we have seen, some states require physicians who are employees of the Department of Corrections to participate in executions, in violation of professional ethical codes. What happens to these physicians when, on ethical grounds, they refuse to participate? We conducted interviews with prison physicians to find out.

Although no cases are known in which physicians have been fired for not participating, some have suffered consequences for their refusal. The following examples illustrate the subtle and overt ramifications for physicians who refuse to assist in the execution process.

When Oklahoma became the first state to legislate lethal injection as its method of execution, Armond Start, M.D., the corrections medical director, used his position to speak out against physician involvement and warned the profession about the need for standards. A few years later, he moved to Texas, where a new director of corrections made changes that threatened the autonomy of health services. Dr. Start left his position. Physician participation in executions was an area of contention.

In Illinois, Ron Shansky, M.D., medical director, obtained verbal agreement from the corrections director that he would not be asked to participate in executions. Subsequently, it was written into Dr. Shansky's employment contract. During the period of this contract, Illinois

---

[43] Anno BJ. Prison Health Care: *Guidelines for the Management of an Adequate Delivery System*. Washington, DC: U.S. Department of Justice; 1992.

prepared to execute a man by lethal injection. The Illinois Attorney General's office insisted that physicians be involved in the execution procedures, because of challenges to the procedures as a violation of the Eighth Amendment prohibition against cruel and unusual punishment. The Attorney General argued that the challenge was strengthened if medical tasks were delegated to people without medical training or skills. Dr. Shansky was consulted about the drugs and lethal doses, but refused to answer the questions. At the time, his position was protected by his employment contract.

After the execution, a new director of corrections was appointed and insisted upon meeting with Dr. Shansky before renewing his annual contract. The director questioned the significance of the clause prohibiting participation in executions and required its removal from the contract. He claimed he would honor a verbal agreement to exempt Dr. Shansky from participating. However, the action represented an attitude that correctional health professionals function only to serve the institution. The medical director saw his autonomy erode and subsequently left his position.

In California, where the death penalty can be implemented by either the gas chamber or lethal injection, regulations call for two physicians in attendance at executions. Department of Corrections officials tacitly expect their employed physicians to be involved, especially those in administrative positions such as chief medical officers. Kim Thorburn, M.D., sought a position as staff physician at San Quentin, the institution with the gas chamber. She informed the chief medical officer that, if hired, she would be unwilling to participate in an execution. The chief medical officer agreed to this condition.

In 1982, Dr. Thorburn was censured by the prison administration for speaking publicly as a prison physician against the nation's first lethal injection execution. Following this experience and after much discussion, the California Medical Association (CMA) passed a resolution to seek legislation that would protect state-employed physicians from sanctions for refusing to participate in executions. Despite support from the CMA, the state's corrections department successfully lobbied for defeat of the bill, and maintained its ability to force state-employed physicians to participate in executions.

After a few years, Dr. Thorburn applied to be chief medical officer at San Quentin. The interview with the warden focussed on the need for physician participation in executions, and the warden stated that the medical officer would be expected to support the staff who carried out the execution. Dr. Thorburn, who held highest rank on a statewide hiring list, was not promoted to vacancies at that prison nor other facilities.

While awaiting another hiring interview, Dr. Thorburn overheard the warden talking about interviewing candidates for chief medical officer. The warden referred to "that doctor and her problem with the death penalty." After notifying the warden's boss about the conversation, Dr. Thorburn was promoted the next day, although the department denied that she had been blackballed. Dr. Thorburn served as chief medical officer at two of the state's prisons before leaving to take a position in a state without the death penalty.

The three physicians in these examples were clear about their professional obligations regarding involvement in executions. They all took stands that brought them in direct conflict with correctional administrators. The support of the medical profession is essential to physicians in these positions.

A few states have chosen to specifically exempt health professionals employed by department of corrections from participating in executions. In New Mexico, a lethal injection state, corrections department regulations state that health care professionals working in correctional facilities cannot participate in any part of the execution procedure "without compromising their professional ethics and their capacity to provide services."[44] In addition, the regulations bar psychiatrists working in correctional facilities from evaluating an inmate's competency for execution.

THE ROLE OF STATE MEDICAL SOCIETIES AND LICENSING BOARDS

Many physicians will continue to participate in executions (some perhaps without enthusiasm) unless there is strong professional pressure combined with state acknowledgement of the professional ethics against medical involvement. Professional pressure is usually exerted through the influence of state medical societies and the regulatory power of state

---

[44] New Mexico Corrections Department, Health Services Standard of Care Number 86/11/02.

licensing boards. We surveyed all state medical societies about their position on physician participation in executions.

In the thirty-six states with death penalty statutes, ten medical societies said that they had written policies opposing physician participation; eighteen medical societies said they had no stated policy, but would defer to the AMA on the issue. Sixteen societies indicated that they would support a physician who refused to participate in executions; twelve states said that they would sanction a physician for participating in executions as a violation of medical ethics. Ten medical societies said that they were aware of state laws regarding physician involvement.

In 1991, the AMA wrote to each state's licensing board to make them aware that the AMA considered physician participation in executions to be a serious violation of the ethical standards of the medical profession. However, to the best of our knowledge, no licensing board has taken action against a physician on these grounds.

5
MEDICAL ETHICS AND PHYSICIAN INVOLVEMENT

Behavior of physicians has been guided historically by the ethical tenets of nonmaleficence (the avoidance of causing harm) and beneficence (the affirmative provision of good). For most of medical history, these two principles defined the ethical limits of clinical practice.

Following the egregious violations of medical ethics perpetrated by physicians during the Nazi regime, the World Medical Association (formed in 1947) adopted two documents which embodied the spirit of the Hippocratic Oath as well as the lessons of the preceding decade.[45] In the wake of Nuremberg revelations, the WMA sought to update the Hippocratic Oath to condemn physician complicity in the commission of antihumanitarian acts at the behest of the state.

The WMA's Declaration of Geneva states that all members of the medical profession must "maintain the utmost respect for human life from its beginning even under threat" and must not use medical knowledge "contrary to the laws of humanity."[46] The International Code of Medical Ethics states that "a physician shall, in all types of medical practice, be dedicated to providing competent medical service in full technical and moral independence, with compassion and respect for human dignity."[47] These documents are perhaps the most explicit statements about the medical profession's obligation to elevate medical ethics over contravening state laws or regulations. Physicians are in large measure governed by their own professional ethics, from which they derive the public trust and societal authority to practice medicine.

Physician involvement in the administration of capital punishment is ethically proscribed because it violates the ethical precepts of the profession. Medicine is a therapeutic and compassionate

---

[45] These were the Declaration of Geneva (1948) and the International Code of Medical Ethics (1949).

[46] World Medical Association. *Handbook of Declarations* 22 (1985).

[47] *Ibid.*

enterprise, and neither of these goals is consistent with physician participation in executions. In this section, we consider the ethical questions posed by the many roles that physicians are asked to play in the execution process.

THE VARIETIES OF MEDICAL INVOLVEMENT

Increasingly, penal authorities have employed the medical profession's evaluative skills and therapeutic techniques to prepare prisoners for execution and to legitimate the act of killing. Although some may propose that the physicians' functions ensure a more "humane" execution, on deeper analysis, the goal appears not to reduce pain, but to maximize efficiency. The major forms of such involvement are set out below:

Medical Evaluation
Physicians have been asked to use their evaluative skills in three ways: clinical assessment of condemned inmates' mental competence for execution, physician examination in preparation for the execution, and clinical monitoring of vital signs during the execution.

Psychiatric Assessment of Competence to be Executed
For at least 300 years, the notion that insane persons should not be executed has been part of Anglo-American law. However, only in 1986 did the U.S. Supreme Court elevate this idea to the status of a constitutional requirement. In *Ford v. Wainwright*, the Court held that the execution of an incompetent person violates the Eighth Amendment proscription against cruel and unusual punishment, and that trial-type procedures are constitutionally necessary to determine competence for execution.[48] However, the Court neither required that psychiatric testimony be part of such hearings nor set forth criteria for the assessment of competence. The role of psychiatrists in such proceedings

---

[48]   477 U.S. 399 (1986).

is ill-defined in American law and has been vigorously contested by medical ethics commentators.[49]

Physical Evaluation in Preparation for the Execution

Physicians also perform pre-execution physical evaluation of patients. As we described in Chapter 4, physicians have provided advice on drugs and helped design protocols for lethal injection executions. Physicians have examined veins for lethal injections and measured height and weight for hangings.

Clinical Monitoring

This evaluative role continues during the execution itself. Twenty-three states specifically require a physician to determine or pronounce death during the administration of capital punishment as mandated in their state statutes or regulations. [See TABLE 2] In order to determine or pronounce death, physicians need to monitor vital signs of the condemned, usually with stethoscopes or electrocardiograms. If the initial attempt to execute the prisoner fails for any reason, a physician may be called upon for advice as to whether additional shocks or lethal chemicals should be administered, or whether the patient should be resuscitated to await a future execution attempt.

In addition, at least twenty-eight states require the presence of a physician, another five claim that a physician "may" be present. [See map of physician participation by state]. Since these laws do not indicate the purpose of the physician presence, one can only surmise that medical expertise is desired by the state to ensure that the procedure runs smoothly, in case something goes awry, or to pronounce death. Mere physician "presence" in the execution chamber risks conveying the message that the execution is countenanced by the medical profession.

The AMA guidelines make a distinction between "pronouncing" death, which they hold to be unethical, and "certifying" death, which they hold to be acceptable. According to the AMA report, whereas pronouncing involves "monitoring the condition of the condemned during the execution and determining at which point the individual has actually died," certifying is "confirming that the individual is dead after another

---

[49] Bloche MG. Psychiatry, capital punishment and the purposes of medicine. *International Journal of Law and Psychiatry* (forthcoming).

person has pronounced or determined that the individual is dead."[50]
Certification of death occurs after the execution is complete, and does not
require the presence of the physician at the site of the execution.

Medical Intervention

Medical intervention on death row pursues both therapeutic and
non-therapeutic purposes. Such intervention can be divided into four
distinct categories: medical treatment that has no bearing on whether a
prisoner is subsequently executed; treatment that restores or maintains
a prisoner's competence for execution; use of clinical methods to subdue
condemned inmates who physically resist execution procedures; and the
use of clinical techniques as part of the physical process of killing.

Medical Care That Does Not Facilitate Execution

Inmates on death row have a constitutionally-protected right to
basic medical treatment.[51] Long-term death row prisoners often have
significant medical needs that can be met without facilitating execution;
such medical care can be clearly distinguished from participation in
execution by the establishment of a doctor-patient relationship, and by
the voluntariness of treatment.

Psychiatric Treatment to Restore or Maintain Competence for Execution

A judicial finding that a prisoner is incompetent to be executed
compels the state to defer execution until competency is restored. In this
clinical context, successful psychiatric treatment, followed by a legal
determination of competence, results in the death of the condemned
person. If the prisoner is not treated, execution is deferred indefinitely,
unless the inmate's mental status improves spontaneously.

The constitutionality of involuntary treatment to restore
competence for execution remains unsettled. In 1990, the U.S. Supreme
Court heard arguments of *Perry v. Louisiana*, which involved a psychotic

---

[50] Council on Ethical and Judicial Affairs. Physician participation in capital
punishment. *Journal of the American Medical Association* 1993;270:365-368.

[51] *Estelle v. Gamble*, 429 U.S. 97 (1976).

PHYSICIAN PARTICIPATION IN EXECUTIONS, AS REQUIRED BY STATE STATUTES AND/OR REGULATIONS

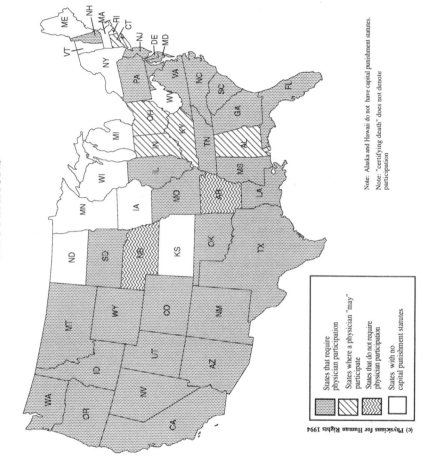

Note: Alaska and Hawaii do not have capital punishment statutes.

Note: "certifying death" does not denote participation

States that require physician participation

States where a physician "may" participate

States that do not require physician participation

States with no capital punishment statutes

(c) Physicians for Human Rights 1994

PHYSICIAN PARTICIPATION IN EXECUTIONS[*]
TABLE 2

[*] S= Mandated by state statutes
R= Mandated by Department of Corrections Regulations

STATE	MD "MUST" BE PRESENT	MD "SHALL" BE PRESENT	MD "MAY" BE PRESENT	DETERMINE OR PRONOUNCE DEATH	MD "MUST" CERTIFY DEATH	MD LISTED AS WITNESS	MD "INVITED TO ATTEND" EXECUTION	STATE STATS. REFER TO D.o.C. REGS. (^)	DEPT. OF CORRECTIONS REGS. NOT AVAILABLE
AL			S					^	NA
AZ	R						S		
AR					R			^	
CA	R			R	R		S		
CO		S		S	S	S			NA
CT			S						NA
DE	R			R	R			^	
FL	R	S		R/S	R	R			
GA	S			S	S				NA
ID	S			S					NA
IL	R/S			S	S				
IN			S						NA
KY			S						NA
LA	R/S			R					
MD	S								NA
MS	S				S	S			NA
MO	R	S		R			S		
MT	S			S					NA
NB									NA
NV	S						S		NA
NH	S			S					NA
NJ	S			S	S				NA
NM	S				S		S		NA
NC	R/S			R	S	S			
OH			S			R			
OK	R			R			S		
OR	R			R			R/S		
PA	g			S		S			NA
SC	R			R	R/S			^	
SD	S			S					NA
TN									NA
TX	R	S		R		S			
UT	S			S		R			NA
VA	R/S			R/S	S				
WA	R/S.			R/S	R				
WY	S			S		S			NA

death row inmate.[52]   The condemned man, Michael Owen Perry, challenged the constitutional validity of a trial judge's order that he be medicated by prison physicians, forcibly if necessary, to render him competent for execution. The justices voided the involuntary medication order without issuing an opinion and sent the case back to the Louisiana courts for reconsideration.

In late 1992, Louisiana's high court held that such involuntary medication constitutes punishment, not therapy, and thereby violates the state's constitutional proscription against "cruel, excessive or unusual punishment."[53]   If appellate courts in other states follow Louisiana's lead, the practice of medicating death row inmates against their will to ensure their competence for execution could disappear without a federal constitutional ruling.

By contrast, **voluntary** treatment that maintains competence for execution is legal, so long as the physician ensures that the patient grasps the legal implications of treatment success. The potentially lifesaving consequences of a psychiatric relapse, as well as the deadly results of treatment success, are central to consent to psychiatric treatment on death row. As such, they should be explained to competent patients in order to comply with the requirement of informed consent.

The arguments against treatment to restore competency are not only legal, but ethical. It seems clear that in most of these instances the physician serves the interests of the state and not those of the patient.

Techniques for Overcoming Physical Resistance

Prison officials may ask a physician to use pharmaceutical or other clinical methods to subdue an inmate who is resisting execution. If sedation is provided in the absence of the inmate's request and consent, the physician becomes a participant in the execution. This type of medical intervention is rather rare.

Clinical Methods as Part of the Execution Process

As we have shown, physicians have also been directly involved in the execution itself, primarily in the process of lethal injections. Cases have been reported in Illinois and Missouri where physicians have

---

[52]   494 U.S. 1015 (1990) (granting certiorari).

[53]   *Perry v. Louisiana*, 610 So. 2d 746 (1992).

inserted intravenous lines and administered lethal injections. Although none of the states that use lethal injection actually require a physician to be the executioner, only New Jersey specifically excludes physicians from that role.

ETHICAL ANALYSIS

Background

The contemporary ethical prohibition against medical participation in capital punishment is deeply rooted in the professional tradition of nonmaleficence. In recent years, physician participation has been condemned by the World Medical Association, the World Psychiatric Association, and national medical societies throughout the industrialized world, including the United States.[54] Some opponents of physician involvement base their objections on their belief that capital punishment is immoral or contrary to international law.[55] Many others, including the American Medical Association, take the position that the morality of the death penalty is a matter of personal conscience but that physician complicity in its administration is nevertheless unethical.

Physician participation in executions represents a significant challenge to morality of the medical profession. For patients and the

---

[54] World Medical Association. Resolution on Physician Participation in Capital Punishment. In: *Handbook of Declarations* 22 (1985).

World Psychiatric Association. *Declaration on the Participation of Psychiatrists in the Death Penalty* (1989).

As of 1989, national medical associations in at least nineteen countries had formally stated their opposition to physician participation in capital punishment. These included the American Medical Association and the medical societies of Japan, France, the Netherlands, Ireland, Denmark, Finland, Iceland, Norway, Sweden, Portugal, Poland, Switzerland, Turkey, New Zealand, Singapore, Peru and Chile. Amnesty International, *Health Professionals and the Death Penalty*, 1989.

[55] This sentiment prevails in Europe, where most nations have ratified a protocol of the European Convention on Human Rights that calls for the death penalty to be abolished. For a comprehensive discussion of the international legal status of the death penalty, see Rodley NS. *The Treatment of Prisoners Under International Law*, UNESCO, Paris, Claredon Press, Oxford 1987.

public, the credibility of physicians is inextricably linked to the medical profession's separation from activities that directly conflict with its central mission. As AMA executive vice president James Todd, M.D., recently said, "When the healing hand becomes the hand inflicting the wound, the world is turned inside out."[56] Society trusts that physicians will work for the benefit of their patients; that trust is threatened by physician participation in executions.

Many commentators have based their opposition to physician participation in executions on the Hippocratic dictum, "first, do no harm." As one physician has written, "Doctors are not executioners. Inflicted death is antithetical to their ancient creed."[57] The Council on Ethical and Judicial Affairs of the AMA notes, "Physician participation in executions contradicts the dictates of the medical profession by causing harm rather than alleviating pain and suffering."[58]

Some people might suggest, however, that physician participation could be construed as compassionate and caring, rather than harmful. Lethal injection, for example, was introduced as a method that would appear to be less excruciating than electrocution, the gallows, or gas. A physician might conclude that given the inevitability of an execution, participation might be ethically acceptable. Although physician participation in some instances may arguably reduce pain, there are many countervailing arguments. First, the purpose of medical involvement may not be to reduce harm or suffering, but to give the surface appearance of humanity. Second, the physician presence also serves to give an aura of medical legitimacy to the procedure. Third, in the larger picture, the physician is taking over some of the responsibility for carrying out the punishment and in this context, becomes the handmaiden of the state as executioner. In return for possible reduction of pain, the physician, in effect, acts under the control of the state, doing harm.

---

[56] Address given by James Todd, M.D., at the opening of the exhibit entitled "The Worth of the Human Being: Medicine in Germany 1918-1945," on November 5, 1992, in Washington, D.C.

[57] Thorburn KM. Doctors and executions. *American Journal of Dermatopathology* 1985;7:87.

[58] Council on Ethical and Judicial Affairs. Physician participation in capital punishment. *Journal of the American Medical Association* 1993;270:365-368.

Physicians are clearly out of place in the execution chamber, and their participation subverts the core of their professional ethics, which require them to "maintain the utmost respect for human life from its beginning even under threat" and to provide "competent medical service in full technical and moral independence, with compassion and respect for human dignity."[59] These insights produce a more subtle and comprehensive prohibition on physician participation than simple reliance upon the Hippocratic dictum of *primum non nocere*. Nevertheless, the maxim, "first, do no harm" represents a powerful, evocative ideal.

Of course, we do not and cannot divorce all medical activities from service to the state. Medical evaluation commonly determines whether persons receive or are denied disability benefits, workers' compensation, tort damages, insurance, and some types of employment. Clinical assessments bear on people's rights to sign contracts, make wills, and otherwise be regarded as autonomous actors. But adjudicating social benefits and facilitating execution are two very different acts.

Moreover, service to society in a manner that exposes individuals to harm can undermine the credibility of medicine as a therapeutic endeavor. This had led medical ethics authorities to conclude that some clinical work on behalf of state purposes is ethically intolerable. Sometimes, this conclusion derives from the illegitimacy of a purported social purpose. Proscriptions against medical evaluation of prisoners' fitness for torture are one such example.[60] In other instances, this conclusion rests on the perception that some state purposes, while arguably legitimate, are so antithetical to the physician's therapeutic role as to be incompatible with it. An example is the waging of war. The use of medical skills to kill enemy soldiers is universally viewed as unethical.

The proscription against physician participation in capital punishment fits into this latter category. Punitive killing is contrary to longstanding professional tradition, which has singled out medically-

---

[59] World Medical Association. International Code of Medical Ethics, *Handbook of Declarations* 22 (1985).

[60] United Nations, *Principles of Medical Ethics Relevant to the Role of Health Personnel, Particularly Physicians, in the Protection of Prisoners and Detainees Against Torture and Other Cruel, Inhuman or Degrading Treatment or Punishment.* U.N. Doc. ST/DPI/801, 1982; and World Medical Association, *Declaration of Tokyo.*

inflicted death as a special concern. In our century, concerns about medical killing have been heightened by awareness of Nazi medical atrocities.[61]   The special status of killing in medical ethics reflects its singular, awesome finality that is different from other harms.

It has been argued that acceptance of the non-provision of life-prolonging treatment, or even euthanasia in some situations, proves that the difference between execution and other harms lacks "categorical force" from a medical ethics perspective.[62]   But withdrawal of life-sustaining technology **at a patient's behest** is consonant with the duty most fundamental to the medical ethics tradition, the obligation to keep faith with patients.   When a physician takes away life sustaining treatment, it is the disease, and not the state, that kills the patient. By contrast, death sentences are not executed to keep faith with the condemned. Even in the unusual case of a defendant who expresses a persisting preference for death, execution is **punishment**, first and foremost.   Physician deference to patient choice with respect to life-sustaining treatment honors the Hippocratic tradition of fidelity to patients. As such, it cannot plausibly be compared to medical complicity in the punitive termination of life by the state.

Defining "Participation"

What activities constitute physician "participation" in capital punishment? The medical ethics authorities that have condemned such participation have, for the most part, failed to address this question. In 1991, at the request of the American College of Physicians, the American Medical Association took a large step toward the formulation of guidelines for physician activities on death row. As we stated earlier, the AMA's House of Delegates, the association's legislative body, instructed the AMA Council on Ethical and Judicial Affairs (CEJA) to develop a definition of participation that included the following prohibited activities:

- selecting lethal injection sites
- starting intravenous lines to serve as ports for lethal injections

---

[61] Proctor R. Racial Hygiene: *Medicine Under the Nazis*, 1988.

[62] Bonnie R. Dilemmas in administering the death penalty: conscientious abstention, professional ethics, and the needs of the legal system. *Law and Human Behavior* 67,76; 1990.

- prescribing or administering pre-execution tranquilizers or other psychotropic agents
- inspecting, testing, or maintaining lethal injection devices
- consulting with or supervising lethal injection personnel
- monitoring vital signs on site or remotely (including monitoring electrocardiograms)
- attending, observing, or witnessing executions as a physician
- providing psychiatric information to certify competence to be executed
- providing psychiatric treatment to establish competence to be executed
- soliciting or harvesting organs for donation by condemned prisoners[63]

In 1992, CEJA issued a report that provides detailed guidance regarding all but the last three activities.[64] Detailed guidelines regarding psychiatric participation in executions were deferred pending consultation with the Ethics Committee of the American Psychiatric Association.

The American College of Physicians, Human Rights Watch, The National Coalition to Abolish the Death Penalty, and Physicians for Human Rights endorse the prohibitions adopted by the AMA's House of Delegates. We offer our own analysis below, by way of clarification and amplification. We divide our discussion into two categories--activities about which there is broad ethical consensus and activities that continue to engender controversy.

Areas of Consensus
Medical Care That Does Not Facilitate Execution

Ethics authorities and commentators are virtually unanimous in their support for the appropriateness of medical care that has no effect on whether or not an inmate is subsequently executed. The health needs

---

[63] Resolution 5, on Defining Physician Participation in State Executions, introduced by the American College of Physicians, 1991 Interim Meeting of the American Medical Association's House of Delegates.

[64] Council on Ethical and Judicial Affairs. Physician participation in capital punishment. *Journal of the American Medical Association* 1993; 270:365-368.

of prisoners, on death row and elsewhere, are too often neglected. Physicians who attend to prisoners often do so under difficult circumstances, with inadequate resources.   Prolonged death row confinement is associated with many physical and mental health problems. As long as informed and competent consent is obtained from inmates in a non-coercive manner, clinical care that does not facilitate execution is both ethical and desirable.

Interventions That Facilitate Execution
        Preparation for execution represents a spectrum of involvement from advising correctional officials on the appropriate techniques for execution to actually preparing or administering lethal injections. All of these activities are ethically inappropriate for physicians and should not be tolerated.
        Physician involvement in physical assessment to prepare for the execution — e.g., examination of potential sites for lethal injection or measurement of height and weight in preparation for hanging — has been uniformly condemned as unethical. These actions have no conceivable therapeutic purpose. The physician who performs them acts literally as the executioner's assistant. These functions are so closely tied to the act of killing as to be ethically indistinguishable from it.
        Physician monitoring of cardiac function, pulse, and respiration during the process of killing has also been uniformly condemned as unethical. Not only does such monitoring lack any therapeutic purpose; it makes physicians into key administrators in the killing process. The monitoring physician's indication that signs of life persist is tantamount to an order for lethal measures to be continued. This intimate causal link between the monitoring of vital signs and the death of the condemned compels the conclusion that such monitoring is unethical for physicians.

Areas of Controversy
Psychiatric Treatment that Restores Competence for Execution
        Treatment that restores death row inmates to competence for execution is widely believed to be unethical. However, some prison psychiatrists contend that it is ethical so long as it is done for the **purpose** of relieving the psychiatric symptoms, rather than for the purpose of killing the inmate. To proponents of this view, the legal consequences of treatment success are ethically irrelevant. Adherents to this view see themselves as acting within the Hippocratic tradition even when

successful treatment leads to the killing of the condemned. In so doing, they distort the Hippocratic commitment into an ethic of indifference to patients as persons. This indifference is underlined by the obviousness of the **penal** function that such treatment serves. However the treating psychiatrist understands his or her role, the ultimate, **public** end furthered by clinical "success" is the execution of the condemned. Psychiatric treatment that has the **effect** of restoring competence for execution should thus, as a rule, be regarded as unethical.

On the other hand, one can imagine circumstances in which an ethic of commitment to patients as whole persons might lead a psychiatrist to consider the legal consequences of therapeutic success and nonetheless decide to treat. For example, a delusional prisoner's self-mutilating behavior or a severely disorganized psychotic inmate's inability to eat invite the judgment that the urgency of relieving agony or forestalling an immediate threat to life outweighs the prospect of execution. This possibility merits an exception to the proscription against treatment that might restore the condemned to competence. But this exception should be sharply limited, to cases of **extreme suffering** or **immediate danger to life.**[65]

Psychiatric Evaluation Bearing on Competence to be Executed
The ethics of psychiatric evaluation in this context have in recent years been a subject of bitter controversy. The AMA, the British Medical Association, and many medical ethics commentators have concluded that such evaluations constitute unethical participation in executions. However, some practitioners of forensic psychiatry (defined as the actions of psychiatrists in assisting the law to carry out some of its responsibilities) dispute this view on the grounds that they have no ethical duty to concern themselves with harm that may result from forensic

---

[65] Anti-psychotic treatment on death row to relieve such suffering is consistent with the emerging consensus that preservation of life should not always take priority over the relief of suffering. See, for example, Council on Ethical and Judicial Affairs. Withholding life-prolonging medical treatment. *Journal of the American Medical Association* 256:1986.

evaluation.[66] They assert that the Hippocratic ethic of commitment to patient well-being is irrelevant to their work because, when doing forensic assessments, they do not function **as physicians**.[67]

This claim ignores the reality that forensic practitioners derive their authority — their franchise to make legally significant distinctions based upon health status — from their training and status as physicians. Forensic practitioners are physicians in the eyes of the public, the courts, and even their examinees. The lines between therapeutic and forensic work are blurry, both in popular understanding and daily practice. Equally worrisome is the open-endedness of the claim that forensic physicians do not function as doctors. If psychiatrists who evaluate competence for execution can say that they are not acting as doctors, why can't internists who select lethal injection sites say the same?

Clinical assessment of an inmate's competence to be executed is unethical, we believe, because it gives the medical profession a decisive role with respect to the final legal obstacle to execution. The proximity between this clinical role and the act of killing casts doctors metaphorically as hangman's aides. On this basis, clinical examination and testimony bearing on competence for execution can be distinguished from other forensic activities that result in harm to the subjects of evaluation.

---

[66] Bloch S. and Chodoff P. *Psychiatric Ethics*. Oxford: Oxford University Press, 1981.

[67] Appelbaum P. The parable of the forensic psychiatrist: ethics and the problem of doing harm. *International Journal of Law and Psychiatry*, 1990.

6
CONCLUSIONS AND RECOMMENDATIONS

In this report, we have examined physician participation in executions. We reviewed ethical standards of conduct and explained the importance of the ethical prohibition against physician involvement. Recent guidelines specify the activities that constitute unethical conduct by physicians in the execution process. In the course of our research, we found that physicians are involved in all methods of executions, especially ones performed by lethal injection, in violation of professional ethical guidelines. Physicians continue to consult on lethal dosages, examine veins, start intravenous lines, witness executions and pronounce death. The threat posed to the moral standing of physicians, and to the public trust that physicians hold, is great. It warrants immediate and decisive action to assure the public, and each patient, that physicians will not use their skills to cause immediate and irreparable harm.

We also discovered that state law and regulation are in direct conflict with established ethical standards regarding physician participation in executions. The majority of death penalty states define a role for physicians in the execution process, from witnessing in an official capacity to monitoring vital signs and pronouncing death. Although many states declare that execution methods are not medical acts, they seek to involve physicians to make the process more "humane"; this is contradictory and a distortion of the physician's role in society.

Our recommendations are geared to eliminate this conflict between medical ethics and the law, and to allow the medical profession to enforce its ethical guidelines.

RECOMMENDATIONS

- The laws and regulations of all death penalty states should incorporate AMA guidelines on physician participation. In particular, laws mandating physician presence and pronouncement of death should be changed to specifically exclude physician participation.
- Laws should not be enacted that facilitate violations of medical ethical standards (such as anonymity clauses). The medical

45

profession cannot regulate and police itself properly if laws protect violators from scrutiny and review.

- All state medical societies should adopt the AMA guidelines on physician participation in executions. Medical societies should inform state medical boards of the seriousness of this violation of medical ethics, and urge that prompt action be taken against violators.

- State medical boards, which are responsible for licensure and discipline, should define physician participation as unethical conduct, and take appropriate action against physicians who violate ethical standards.

STATE MEDICAL SOCIETY POSITIONS ON PHYSICIAN PARTICIPATION IN EXECUTIONS
TABLE 3

State Medical Society	written policy, oppose MD partici pation	No policy, defer to AMA policy	Support MD who refuses to partici pate	Sanctio ns MD's that partici pate	inter- pretion of law: MD partici pates
AL	NO	YES	NO	NO	N/A
AZ	NO	N/A	NO	NO	NO
AR	YES	NO	N/A	NO	NO
CA	YES	NO	YES	YES	YES
CO	NO	N/A	NO	NO	N/A
CT	NO	NO	NO	NO	N/A
DE	NO	YES	NO	YES	NO
FL	NO	YES	NO	NO	YES
GA	NO	YES	YES	N/A	NO
ID	NO	YES	NO	NO	NO
IL	YES	NO	YES	N/A	YES
IN	NO	YES	NO	NO	NO
KY	NO	YES	YES	NO	NO
LA	NO	NO	NO	NO	NO
MD	NO	YES	YES	YES	NO
MS	NO	YES	YES	NO	YES
MO	NO	YES	YES	YES	YES
MT	NO	NO	N/A	N/A	N/A
NB	NO	NO	N/A	N/A	NO
NV	NO	YES	NO	NO	NO
NH	YES	NO	YES	YES	NO
NJ	YES	NO	YES	YES	NO
NM	NO	YES	YES	N/A	YES
NC	YES	NO	NO	NO	YES
OH	NO	YES	NO	NO	NO
OK	NO	YES	YES	YES	NO
OR	YES	NO	YES	YES	YES
PA	NO	YES	YES	YES	YES
SC	NO	YES	N/A	N/A	NO
SD	NO	NO	N/A	N/A	N/A
TN	NO	NO	N/A	N/A	N/A
TX	YES	NO	NO	NO	NO
UT	YES	NO	YES	YES	NO
VA	NO	YES	YES	YES	NO
WA	YES	NO	YES	YES	NO
WY	NO	YES	N/A	N/A	YES

*Data compiled as of February 1993.
N/A either denotes society was not able to reply or information was not made available.

APPENDIX

ALABAMA

Method of Execution: electrocution. (Article 15-18-82 of *Criminal Procedure*; Punishment is to be inflicted by electrocution.)

State Statute Regarding Physicians' Role: Details of execution procedures to be determined by the Commissioner of Corrections. "Persons who may be present;" (c) Two (2) physicians, including the prison physician. In 1991 a bill to replace electrocution with lethal injection was considered and rejected by the State Legislature. The bill did not mention the role of medical personnel. (Article 15-18-84 of *Criminal Procedure*.)

Department of Corrections Regulations Regarding Physicians' Role: The Alabama Department of Corrections refused to provide the regulations and refused to provide the grounds for its refusal in writing. (Phone conversation on July 7, 1992 with Horace Lynn, Assistant Counsel at the Department of Corrections.)

State Medical Society's Position: The Medical Association of the State of Alabama doesn't have a policy on physician participation in executions; they defer to the AMA. As the situation has not arisen, they have neither sanctioned nor assisted members for participating or not in an execution. They are not aware of whether or not state law mandates physician involvement.

ARIZONA

Method of Execution: lethal gas or lethal injection. (Article 13-704 of *Criminal Code Title 13*)

   A.   The penalty of death shall be inflicted by an intravenous injection of a substance or substances in a lethal quantity sufficient to cause death, under the supervision of the state department of corrections.

   B.   A defendant who is sentenced to death for an offense committed before November 23, 1992 shall choose either lethal injection or lethal gas at least twenty days before the execution date. If the defendant fails to choose either lethal injection or lethal gas, the penalty of death shall be inflicted by lethal injection.

State Statute Regarding Physicians' Role: "Persons present at execution..." The superintendent of the state prison shall invite a physician. (Article 13-705 of *Criminal Code Title 13*)
Department of Corrections Regulations Regarding Physicians' Role: The Department of Corrections' regulations stipulate that a physician should be present to operate the heart monitor.
(Arizona State Prison Complex-Florence Internal Management Procedure (IMP) 500 - "Execution Procedures": §5.5.3.)
State Medical Society's Position: The Arizona Medical Association has no position on physician participation in executions. As their interpretation of state law does not require physician involvement, the issue of whether or not they sanction or assist members who do or don't is moot.

ARKANSAS

Method of Execution: lethal injection. (Article 5-4-617 of *Survey of Arkansas Law - Criminal Procedure*, "Method of Execution" provides the following details: Punishment to be inflicted "by continuous intravenous injection of lethal quality...until the defendant's death is *pronounced* according to *accepted standards of medical practice*." In addition, the 1987 statutes allow for those defendants sentenced prior to July 4, 1983 to choose either electrocution or lethal injection.)
State Statute Regarding Physicians' Role: Specific details regarding witnesses and medical personnel are determined by the Director of the Department of Corrections.
Department of Corrections Regulations Regarding Physicians' Role: The Department of Corrections provided a one-page "Procedures for Executions;" the document stipulates that "a death ruling will be made by the State Medical Examiner's Office following the execution."
State Medical Society's Position: The Arkansas Medical Society has a policy statement against medical participation in executions but has no procedures to discipline those who do. The Society interprets the state law as not requiring medical participation in executions.

CALIFORNIA

Method of Execution: lethal gas or lethal injection. (Assembly Bill 2405—Amendment to Article 3604 of *Penal Code*). Punishment of death shall be inflicted by the administration of a lethal gas or by an intravenous injection of a substance or substances in a lethal quantity sufficient to cause death. Persons sentenced to death shall have the opportunity, as specified, to elect to have the punishment imposed by lethal gas or lethal injection. This choice shall be made in writing. If a person under sentence of death does not choose either lethal gas or lethal injection within 10 days, the penalty of death shall be imposed by lethal gas.

State Statute Regarding Physicians' Role: "The warden of the State Prison where execution (takes place) must be present and must *invite* the presence of two physicians..." (Article 3605 "Witness to Execution".)

Department of Corrections Regulations Regarding Physicians' Role: The state execution procedures, provided by the Department of Corrections, stipulate the presence of the Chief Medical Officer and one additional physician. For their role, as per the regulations, see "Legal Perspective." (San Quentin Institution Procedures.)

State Medical Society's Position: The California Medical Association opposes medical participation in executions, has a procedure to discipline those who disobey and to assist those who need assistance as a result of their refusal to participate. The Association interprets the state statute as requiring physicians to participate in executions.

COLORADO

Method of Execution: lethal injection. (Article 16-11-401 of *Colorado Revised Statutes, 1989 Supplement,* "Method;" Death Penalty to be inflicted by lethal injection.)

State Statute Regarding Physicians' Role: The execution shall be performed in the appointed room or place..."by a person selected by the Executive Director (of the Department of Corrections) and trained to administer intravenous injections.... Death shall be pronounced by a licensed physician or coroner according to accepted medical standards." (Article 16-11-402 of *Colorado Revised Statutes, 1989 Supplement,* "Implements.")

A physician shall be present. (Article 16-11-404 of *Colorado Revised Statutes, 1989 Supplement,* "Witnesses.")

Immediately after the execution, a postmortem examination shall be made by the attending physician. (Article 16-11-405 of *Colorado Revised Statutes, 1989 Supplement,* "Record and certificate of execution.")

Department of Corrections Regulations Regarding Physicians' Role:
We were unable to obtain a copy of the regulations. According to a letter
from the Executive Director of the Colorado Department of Corrections,
"documents governing the process to be put into place and activated to
conduct an execution are confidential to the Department and made
available only to those who have a 'need to know.'" (June 9, 1992 letter
from Frank O. Gunter.) Our subsequent letter and phone messages
requesting the legal grounds for confidentiality went unanswered.
State Medical Society's Position: The Colorado Medical Society does not
have a policy regarding physician participation in executions, but they are
looking into it. They are unaware of state law regarding this issue.

CONNECTICUT

Method of Execution: electrocution.
State Statute Regarding Physicians' Role: The warden of the
Correctional Institution in Somers appoints the executioner. "The
following persons *may* be present...the physician of the Connecticut
Correctional Institution, Somers..." (Article 54-100 of *Criminal Procedure*,
"Electrocution.")
Department of Corrections Regulations Regarding Physicians' Role:
According to a letter from the Department of Corrections, the State of
Connecticut does not have departmental regulations regarding
executions, due to the fact that the last execution in the state took place
in 1960. (June 19, 1992 letter from Leo C. Arnoe.)
The State Medical Society's Position: The Connecticut State Medical
Society does not have a position on physicians' participation in execution
and is not aware of the law's requirements.

DELAWARE

Method of Execution: lethal injection. (Article 4209 (f) of *Delaware Code
Revised 1974-1988 Supplement*, "Method and imposition of sentence of
death" specifies lethal injection as the mode of execution and states: "The
administration of the required lethal substances...shall *not* be construed to
be the *practice of medicine* and any pharmacist or pharmaceutical supplier
is authorized to dispense drugs (to the Commissioner of the Department
of Corrections) *without prescription*. If lethal injection is held to be
unconstitutional or infeasible, punishment is to be inflicted by hanging.)

Department of Corrections Regulations Regarding Physicians' Role:
The Delaware Department of Corrections Policies and Procedures stipulate that in the case of execution by lethal injection, a physician or physicians confirm death. If the execution is by hanging, the procedure is that the physician(s) will determine that death has occurred after the inmate dropped through the trap. (Department of Corrections, State of Delaware, Policies and Procedures Number 750, Execution Procedures.)

Our letter to the Delaware Department of Corrections went unanswered. Following repeated phone messages, we were eventually told that the information was confidential. We requested to receive the denial in writing with the citation of legal grounds for the confidentiality. We have not received this information. A copy of the document was obtained through further research.

State Medical Society's Position: The Medical Society of Delaware does not have a policy statement on the role of physicians in executions, but it defers on this issue to the American Medical Association.

FLORIDA

Method of Execution: electrocution. (Article 922-10 of *Criminal Procedures and Corrections*, "Execution of Death Sentence;" inflicted by electrocution and overseen by the warden of the State Prison, who designates the executioner.)

State Statute Regarding Physicians' Role: "A qualified physician shall be present and announce when death has been inflicted." (Article 922-11 of *Criminal Procedures and Corrections*, "Regulation of Execution" (2).)

NOTE: A bill to replace electrocution with lethal injection was considered and rejected by the State Legislature in 1991.

Department of Corrections Regulations Regarding Physicians' Role:
The Florida State Prison Operating Procedure, provided to us by the Florida Department of Corrections, specifies that a physician and a physician's assistant are to be among the five people (in addition to the condemned person) present in the execution chamber immediately prior and throughout the execution. An additional physician is in the witness room. (Florida State Prison Operating Procedure.) For more details, see: "Legal Perspective."

State Medical Society's Position: The Florida Medical Association does not have a policy regarding physician participation in executions. They defer to the AMA on this issue, but are not necessarily in agreement. They neither sanction nor assist members who do or don't participate in executions. They are aware of state statutes regarding physician involvement.

GEORGIA

Method of Execution: electrocution.
State Statute Regarding Physicians' Role: At least three executioners, two physicians "to determine when death supervenes" and electricians are required to attend. (Article 17-10-41 of *Criminal Procedure*, "Persons required to be present at executions.")
Executioners and attending physicians certify execution to the court clerk. (Article 17-10-42 of *Criminal Procedure*, "Preparation and filing of certification." Article 17-10-44 of *Criminal Procedure*, "Death chamber apparatus, etc.," describes what is needed to carry out execution by electrocution.)
Department of Corrections Regulations Regarding Physicians' Role:
We were unable to obtain regulations. Our repeated written and phone messages to the effect were ignored. (Letters on June 4 and July 20, 1992, phone calls on June 26, July 16, and July 20.)
State Medical Society's Position: The Medical Association of Georgia has no policy statement on physicians' role in executions because the Society defers on this issue to the position taken by the American Medical Association.

IDAHO

Method of Execution: lethal injection.
State Statute Regarding Physicians' Role: [Death is] inflicted by lethal injection "until death is pronounced by a (licensed) physician in accordance with accepted medical standards." The statute contains language claiming that lethal injection is "not a medical procedure" and that chemicals can be dispensed to the Director of the Department of Corrections without a prescription. In addition, the Director is given a role in determining the mode of execution; if it is deemed that lethal injection cannot be administered in a "reasonable" manner (i.e. without causing suffering) a firing squad will be used. Finally, "infliction of punishment by lethal injection shall not be construed to be the practice

of medicine." (Article 19-2716 of *Idaho Code - 1987 Revision*, "Infliction of Death Penalty.")
Department of Corrections Regulations Regarding Physicians' Role: The Department of Corrections informed us that there was no administrative policy on the department level due to the fact that the last execution was carried out in 1957. There exists, however, a detailed, confidential execution guide of the Idaho Maximum Security Institution, which is where executions orders would be carried out. According to the letter, the document is protected from public disclosure by Idaho Code section 9-340 (35). (July 2, 1992 letter from Karol T. Phillips, Sr. Administrative Assistant, State of Idaho Department of Corrections.)
State Medical Society's Position: The Idaho Medical Association has no policy statement on physicians' role in executions because the Society defers on this issue to the position taken by the American Medical Association.

INDIANA

Method of Execution: electrocution. (Article 35-38-6-1 of *Criminal Law and Procedure*, Manner and time of execution; Punishment is to be inflicted by electrocution. The warden, or persons designated by the warden, shall serve as executioner(s).)
State Statute Regarding Physicians' Role: "Who may be present" includes the prison physician. (Article 35-38-6-6 of *Criminal Law and Procedure*.)
State Medical Society's Position: The Indiana State Medical Association does not have a policy regarding physician participation in executions; they defer to the AMA on this issue. Though the issue has yet to arise, it would be up to the county and state medical boards to determine whether or not to sanction or provide support to a member who did or did not violate this policy. They interpret the law as not requiring physician involvement and are themselves opposed to physician involvement.

ILLINOIS

Method of Execution: lethal injection. (Article 119-5 of *Criminal Law and Procedure*, "Execution of Death Sentence;" (a) Inflicted by lethal injection until death is pronounced by a licensed physician according to accepted medical standards.

State Statute Regarding Physicians' Role: Execution is to be conducted in the presence of two (2) physicians who, along with other witnesses, shall certify that the execution has taken place. The identity of executioners and other participants shall remain confidential. (Article 119-5 of *Criminal Law and Procedure*, "Execution of Death Sentence;" (d), (e).)

Department of Corrections Regulations Regarding Physicians' Role: The Illinois Department of Corrections Execution Procedure, received from the Department, refers to "a medically trained person," "a Health Care Unit Member," and "qualified health care personnel," ascribing them specific roles.

State Medical Society's Position: The Illinois State Medical Society has a policy against physician participation in executions. They wouldn't necessarily sanction a member who participated in an execution, but would provide support for a member who declined to do so. Their interpretation of the law is that a physician is required to pronounce death.

KENTUCKY

Method of Execution: electrocution. (Article 431.220 of *Kentucky Penal Code*, "Execution of Death Sentence;" punishment inflicted by electrocution.)

State Statute Regarding Physicians' Role: "Persons who may attend executions" includes the physician of the penitentiary. (Article 431-250 of *Kentucky Penal Code*.)

Department of Corrections Regulations Regarding Physicians' Role: Kentucky has not executed an inmate since 1962. According to a letter from the Commissioner of Corrections, a new set of procedures was being drafted as of July 92.

State Medical Society's Position: The Kentucky Medical Association does not have a policy regarding physician participation in executions. They feel they would probably defer to the AMA on this issue. Disciplinary matters are referred to a judicial committee; they would probably provide support to a member who declined to participate in an execution. They are not aware of state law regarding physician involvement.

LOUISIANA

Method of Execution: lethal injection. (Article 569 of *Revised Statutes*, "Place for execution; manner of execution;" Every sentence executed on or after September 15, 1991 shall be carried out by lethal injection.)
State Statute Regarding Physicians' Role: No licensed health care professional "shall be *compelled to administer a lethal injection*." (Article 569 of *Revised Statutes*, "Place for execution; manner of execution;" (c).)
Executions are to take place in the presence of the coroner of the parish of West Feliciana or his deputy and a physician summoned by the warden of the state penitentiary at Angola.
Department of Corrections Regulations Regarding Physicians' Role: The regulations provided by the Department of Public Safety and Corrections list a physician as one of the four people to be present in the execution room during the execution. One of the four people is "a competent person selected by the warden to administer the lethal injection." (Department of Public Safety and Corrections - Department Regulation No. 10-25: §G(2).)
State Medical Society's Position: Unofficially, the Louisiana State Medical Society is against physician participation in executions. They don't necessarily defer to the AMA on this issue. They would not sanction a member who participated in an execution; they might provide assistance to one who declined to do so. They interpret the law as not requiring physician involvement.

MARYLAND

Method of Execution: lethal gas. (Article 27,73 of *Annotated Code of the Public General Laws of Maryland*, "Death Chamber, conduct of executions;" punishment is to be inflicted by lethal gas....)
State Statute Regarding Physicians' Role: Punishment is to be...conducted by the warden or his designee, in the presence of "...the physician of the penitentiary or his assistant..." (Article 27,73 of *Annotated Code of the Public General Laws of Maryland*, "Death Chamber, conduct of executions.")
Department of Corrections Regulations Regarding Physicians' Role:

According to a fax message from the Executive Assistant at the Maryland Department of Public Safety and Correctional Services, the state of Maryland does not have departmental procedures for executions.

State Medical Society's Position: The Medical & Chirurgical Faculty of the State of Maryland defers to the AMA on the issue of physician participation in executions. They would both discipline and assist members who either participated or declined to participate in an execution. Maryland does not require physician involvement in executions.

MISSISSIPPI

Method of Execution: lethal injection or lethal gas. (Article 99-19-51 of *Criminal Procedures*, "Infliction of sentence;" punishment is inflicted by lethal injection or by lethal gas.)

State Statute Regarding Physicians' Role: Lethal injection "shall not be construed to be the practice of medicine or nursing." Pharmacists may dispense drugs to the state executioner without a prescription. (Article 99-19-53 of *Criminal Procedures*, "Execution of death sentence.")

The commissioner secures the presence of at least one, but not more than two physicians. The executioner, Commissioner and physicians prepare and sign the death certificate. (Article 99-19-55 of *Criminal Procedures*, "Witnesses, certificate of execution...;" (2) and (3).)

Department of Corrections Regulations Regarding Physicians' Role: Despite a written request and repeated phone messages left with the office of the Commissioner of the Department of Corrections, we were unable to obtain either a copy of the regulations or an explanation of why our request was ignored.

State Medical Society's Position: The Mississippi State Medical Association does not have a policy regarding physician participation in executions; they defer to the AMA. They would provide support to a member who declined to participate but probably would not discipline him or her because they interpret state law as only requiring a physician to declare death.

MISSOURI

Method of Execution: lethal gas or lethal injection. (Article 546.720 of *1990 Cum Pocket Part*, "Manner of Execution," Punishment of death shall be by administration of lethal gas or by means of the administration of lethal injection.

State Statute Regarding Physicians' Role: The chief administrative officer of the correctional institute shall "invite the presence of a physician." (Article 546-740 of *1990 Cum Pocket Part*, "Witnesses.")

Department of Corrections Regulations Regarding Physicians' Role: The Director of the Department of Corrections in his June 25, 1992 letter stated that copies of regulations governing executions "will not be forwarded" for "reasons of safety for staff and inmates." In his letter, he provided some of the details of the existing departmental document. According to his summary, "the inmate is placed on a gurney and the IV is set or put into place by medical staff... The heart and other vital signs are monitored electronically by a medical staff person. The inmate is pronounced dead by a physician, and the blinds to the witness viewing area are closed."

A recently published book provides a few more details as to the nature of a physician's involvement. The physician is present in the execution chamber and monitors the dying inmate's heart from behind a screen, located about a foot away from the gurney. (Stephen Trombley, "The Execution Protocol," Crown Publishers, New York 1992. Caption under a photograph depicting the execution chamber.)

State Medical Society's Position: The Missouri State Medical Association does not have a policy regarding physician participation in executions; they defer to the AMA. If a member acted in contravention of this policy, they would consider it an ethics violation and proceed accordingly; they would assist members who declined to participate in executions. Such an occasion has yet to arise. Their interpretation of the law is that Missouri mandates physician participation.

MONTANA

Method of Execution: hanging or lethal injection. (Article 46-19-103 of *Criminal Procedure*, "Execution of the Death Sentence," (3); Punishment is to be inflicted by hanging or, at the election of the defendant, by lethal injection...)

State Statute Regarding Physicians' Role: Punishment is to be inflicted..."until a licensed physician pronounces that the defendant is dead according to accepted standards of medical practice." The warden selects the executioner. Executions by lethal injection must be carried out by a person "trained to administer the injection." This person "need not be a physician, registered nurse or licensed practical nurse..." (Article 46-19-103 of *Criminal Procedure,* "Execution of the Death Sentence;" (3), (5), and (6).)

Department of Corrections Regulations Regarding Physicians' Role: A June 15 letter from the Department of Corrections stated that "Montana corrections regards its executions procedures manual as a confidential document." Our written request for the grounds for the confidentiality, followed by repeated phone messages, were never answered.

State Medical Society's Position: The Montana Medical Association has a policy that a physician not be compelled to participate in an execution, but it is not in writing. A situation has not yet arisen where the society has either sanctioned or supported a member for participating or not in an execution. They are unaware of state law regarding physician involvement.

NEBRASKA

Method of Execution: electrocution. (Article 25.29-2532 of *Criminal Procedure,* "Mode of inflicting punishment;" punishment is inflicted by electrocution. The Warden, or, in the case he is incapacitated, the Deputy Warden serves as the executioner, unless the warden designates a "competent" executioner (witnesses, physicians, and pronouncement of death are not mentioned).)

Department of Corrections Regulations Regarding Physicians' Role: Despite repeated written and phone requests addressed to the Director of the Department of Correctional Services, we were unable to obtain a copy of the regulations governing executions.

State Medical Society's position: The Nebraska Medical Association has no policy statement on physicians' role in executions.

NEVADA

Method of Execution: lethal injection. (Article 176.355 of *Revised Statutes Volume #7,* "Execution of Death Penalty;" (1) Judgement is to be inflicted by lethal injection.)

State Statute Regarding Physicians' Role: The Director of the Department of Prisons selects the lethal chemicals after consulting with the *state health officer*. The Director must *invite* a competent physician to be present at the execution. (Article 176.355 of *Revised Statutes Volume #7*, "Execution of Death Penalty;" (2)(b),(d).)

Department of Corrections Regulations Regarding Physicians' Role: The Director of the Department of Corrections in his June 16 letter refused to provide us with a copy of Nevada's regulations governing executions, "due to confidentiality." Our written and telephone requests for providing the basis for the confidentiality have been ignored.

State Medical Society's Position: The Nevada State Medical Association does not have a policy regarding physician participation in executions. As the issue has not arisen in Nevada for a long time, they believe they would defer to the AMA. As they interpret the law to not require physician involvement (though a physician may be *invited to attend*), the question regarding sanction or providing a member with assistance is moot.

NEW HAMPSHIRE

Method of Execution: lethal injection. (Article 630:5 XIII. of *1989 Criminal Supplement*, "When the penalty of death is imposed..." punishment is inflicted by lethal injection...until death is pronounced by a licensed physician "according to accepted standards of medical practice...")

State Statute Regarding Physicians' Role: Lethal injection is performed by a person selected by the commissioner and trained to administer the injection. This person "need not be a physician, registered nurse, or licensed practical nurse..." Lethal injection "shall not be construed to be the practice of medicine..." Pharmacists are authorized to dispense the drugs to the commissioner without a prescription. (Articles 630:5 XV. and XVI. of *1989 Criminal Supplement.*)

Department of Corrections Regulations Regarding Physicians' Role: According to a June 10, 1992 letter from the Commissioner of the Department of Corrections, New Hampshire, a state where the most recent execution took place in 1939, does not have regulations for the administration of executions.

State Medical Society's Position: The New Hampshire Medical Society is opposed to physician participation in executions. Though the situation has yet to arise, a member who contravenes the Society policy would be dealt with by its jurisprudence committee and possibly dropped from the society, while a member who declined to participate in an execution would receive the society's assistance. Their interpretation of the law is that it does not require physician involvement.

NEW JERSEY

Method of Execution: lethal injection. (Article 2C:49-2 of *Criminal Justice Code*, Administration of punishment; punishment is inflicted by lethal injection.)

State Statute Regarding Physicians' Role: Prior to the injection of lethal substances, "the person shall be sedated by a licensed physician, registered nurse, or *other qualified personnel...*" (Article 2C:49-2 of *Criminal Justice Code*, Administration of punishment.)

Lethal injection "shall not be construed to be the practice of medicine..." Pharmacists are authorized to dispense drugs to the commissioner without a prescription. The commissioner must designate persons who are "qualified to administer injections and who are familiar with medical procedures, *other than licensed physicians*, as executioners. (Article 2C:49-3 of *Criminal Justice Code*, "Determination of substances and procedure..." (a), (b).)

"Persons authorized to be present;" includes two licensed physicians. (Article 2C:49-7 of *Criminal Justice Code*.)

Immediately after the execution an examination of the body shall be made by the licensed physicians attending the execution. (Article 2C:49-8 of *Criminal Justice Code*, "Examination and report; certificate.")

Department of Corrections Regulations Regarding Physicians' Role: According to a staff member at the office of the Assistant Commissioner, Division of Adult Institutions, New Jersey does not have departmental regulations and procedures on capital punishment.

State Medical Society's Position: The Medical Association of New Jersey has a policy statement against physicians' participation in executions. The Society has developed procedures to discipline its members who violate the policy and procedures to assist members who refuse to participate in executions.

NEW MEXICO

Method of Execution: lethal injection. (Article 31-14-11 of *New Mexico Statutes 1978 Volume #6*, "Punishment of Death; how inflicted;" manner of inflicting punishment is lethal injection; execution is supervised by the Warden of the State Penitentiary.)

State Statute Regarding Physicians' Role: The warden must invite the presence of a physician." (Article 31-14-15 of *New Mexico Statutes 1978 Volume #6*, "Who may be present.")[68]

Department of Corrections Regulations Regarding Physicians' Role: According to a June 12, 1992, letter from the office of the Secretary of the Corrections Department, New Mexico has no procedures for executions, due to the fact that the most recent execution took place in 1960.

State Medical Society's Position: The New Mexico Medical Society has no policy statement on physicians' role in executions because the Society defers on this issue to the position taken by the American Medical Association.

NORTH CAROLINA

Method of Execution: lethal gas or lethal injection. (Article 15-187 of *Criminal Procedure*, "Death by lethal gas or drugs;" states: "Death by electrocution is hereby abolished...Lethal gas is substituted therefor, except that the defendant chooses lethal injection..." (defendant must choose five (5) days prior to execution date). 15-187 amended in 1983 as follows: "Warden may obtain and employ the drugs necessary to carry out the provisions of this act...")

State Statute Regarding Physicians' Role: Witnesses include the surgeon or physician of the penitentiary. (Article 15-190 of *Criminal Procedure*, "Who shall be present...") The warden and surgeon or physician of the penitentiary certify the fact of execution. (Article 15-192 of *Criminal Procedure*, "Certificate of death.")

---

[68] A document issued by the Medical Director of the Office of Health Services of the Corrections Department prohibits any health care professional working in the Corrections Department to participate in any part of the execution procedure. (*Standard of Care*, Topic: Executions, Number: 86/11/02)

Department of Corrections Regulations Regarding Physicians' Role:
The Department of Corrections Research File, in the chapter entitled
"Methods of Execution in North Carolina" states that when lethal
injection is used, "a physician, whose sole function is to pronounce the
inmate dead, watches from the control room. After five to ten minutes,
he goes to the inmate, listens for heart sounds, checks his pupil response
and pronounces him dead. The physician leaves the chamber, the
witnesses are escorted to the elevators and the body is removed." When
asphyxiation by lethal gas is used, "a heart monitor is attached to the
inmate which can be read in the control room by a staff member and a
physician." (Department of Corrections Research File: "Methods of
Execution in North Carolina.")

State Medical Society's Position: The North Carolina Medical Society has
a policy statement against physicians' participation in executions. The
Society has not developed procedures to discipline its members who
violate the policy nor procedures to assist members who refuse to
participate in executions.

OHIO

Method of Execution: electrocution or lethal injection. (Article 2949.22
of *Crimes—Procedure*, "Execution of the Death Sentence;" punishment is
inflicted by electrocution or lethal injection. The warden or his deputy
shall be the executioner.)

State Statute Regarding Physicians' Role: Physicians of the penitentiary
shall be present [at executions]. (Article 2949.25 of *Crimes—Procedure*,
"Attendance at execution;" (d).)

Department of Corrections Regulations Regarding Physicians' Role:
According to a document provided by the Ohio Department of
Rehabilitation and Correction, at the execution of the death penalty, as
witnesses in or about the vicinity of the execution chamber are included,
among others: "Such number of physicians of the institution where the
execution is to be conducted as the superintendent thinks necessary."
(Department of Rehabilitation and Correction Rule No. 5120-9-54:
"Attendance at execution.")

State Medical Society's Position: The Ohio State Medical Association has
no policy statement on physicians' role in executions because the Society
defers on this issue to the position taken by the American Medical
Association.

OKLAHOMA

Method of Execution: lethal injection. (Article 1014 of *Crimes &
Punishments Title 21 681 to 930*, "Manner of Inflicting Punishment of
Death" is by lethal injection administered "...until death is pronounced by
a licensed physician according to accepted standards of medical practice."
State Statute Regarding Physicians' Role: The Warden must invite the
presence of a physician. (Article 1015 of *Crimes & Punishments Title 21 681
to 930*,"Persons who may be present.")
Department of Corrections Regulations Regarding Physicians' Role:
Our letter to the Director of the Oklahoma Department of Corrections
requesting a copy of the departmental regulations, followed by several
phone calls, was ignored.   The Department of Corrections Policy
Statement No. OP-090901: "Procedures for the Execution of Inmates
Sentenced to Death" was quoted, however, in a recent British book. The
document states: The Chief Medical Officer of the Penitentiary, or the
Medical Director of the Department [of Corrections], or a physician
designated by the Warden must be present [at the execution; and after
the catheter has been inserted] the examining physician shall inspect the
catheter and monitoring equipment and determine that the fluid will flow
into the vein... The execution shall be by means of a continuous,
intravenous administration of a lethal quantity of sodium thiopental
combined with either tubo-curarine or succinylcholine chloride or
potassium chloride which is an ultrashort-acting barbiturate combination
with a chemical paralytic agent. The Department Medical Director shall
order a sufficient quantity of the substance... (Passage cited in: British
Medical Association, *Medicine Betrayed: The Participation of Doctors in
Human Rights Abuses*, 1992, p. 112.)
State Medical Society's Position: The Oklahoma State Medical
Association has no policy statement on physicians' role in executions
because the Society defers on this issue to the position taken by the
American Medical Association.

OREGON

Method of Execution: lethal injection. (Article 137.473 of *Oregon Revised
Statutes Vol #3 Penal Code Chapter 131-170*, "Means of inflicting death;

place and procedures; acquisition of lethal substance;" (1) Punishment is inflicted by lethal injection...)

State Statute Regarding Physicians' Role: (1) ...the superintendent shall "invite the presence of one or more physicians..." (2) The person administering the injection "shall not thereby be considered to be engaged in the practice of medicine." (3)(a) Pharmacists may provide the lethal substances upon written order of the Director of the Department of Corrections accompanied by a copy of the court's judgement of death. (Article 137.473 of *Oregon Revised Statutes Vol #3 Penal Code Chapter 131-170*, "Means of inflicting death; place and procedures; acquisition of lethal substance.")

Department of Corrections Regulations Regarding Physicians' Role: According to the regulations provided by the Oregon Department of Corrections, "the selection of the executioner(s) will be the joint responsibility of the superintendent and the health services manager of the Oregon State Penitentiary. (a) All medically-related issues relating to lethal injection shall be the responsibility of the Oregon State Penitentiary health services manager. The document further stipulates that the Oregon State Penitentiary health services manager {superintendent} will identify one or more physicians who will be responsible for observing the execution process and examining the condemned after the lethal substance(s) has been administered to ensure that death has been induced. The superintendent shall be present at the execution and shall invite the presence of: One or more physicians as identified above... And finally the document states: "The intravenous administration of the chemicals will be maintained until death is pronounced by the licensed physician(s)." (Capital Punishment (Death by Lethal Injection)": OAR 291-24-005 through OAR 291-24-095.)

State Medical Society's Position: The Oregon Medical Association has a policy statement against physicians' participation in executions. The Society has developed procedures to discipline its members who violate the policy and procedures to assist members who refuse to participate in executions.

PENNSYLVANIA

Method of Execution: lethal injection. (Article 2121.1 of *Penal & Correctional Inst.*, "Method of execution;" Punishment is inflicted by lethal injection...)

State Statute Regarding Physicians' Role: Punishment is inflicted... until death is pronounced by a licensed physician. Lethal substances are approved by the Department of Corrections.
(Article 2121.1 of *Penal & Correctional Inst.*, "Method of execution.")
Department of Corrections Regulations Regarding Physicians' Role:
Claiming confidentiality, Pennsylvania declined to provide regulations regarding executions.
State Medical Society's Position: The Pennsylvania Medical Society has no policy statement on physicians' role in executions because the Society defers on this issue to the position taken by the American Medical Association.

SOUTH CAROLINA

Method of Execution: electrocution. (Article 24-3-530 of *Code of Laws of South Carolina*, "Method;" punishment is inflicted by electrocution. Execution is directed by the Commissioner of the Department of Corrections.)
State Statute Regarding Physicians' Role: "Witnesses" mentions "necessary staff." "Certification" states "Executioner and the attending physician shall certify the fact of such execution to the (court clerk)." (Articles 24-3-550 and 24-3-560 of *Code of Laws of South Carolina*.)
Department of Corrections Regulations Regarding Physicians' Role:
Two physicians are included among the individuals that will be present when an execution is carried out (one in the execution chamber and one in the witness area). (The Department of Corrections' "Execution Procedures" paragraph 6.c.) The regulations stipulate that "...the Director of the Division of Health Services will: (1) Ensure that physicians are present during the execution to certify that the execution was carried out." The warden will "request physician to confirm death after electrical sequence... The inmate will be pronounced dead by the physician. (South Carolina Dept. of Corrections Policy No. 1500.31 (15/31) — "Execution Procedures.")
State Medical Society's Position: The South Carolina Medical Association does not have a policy regarding physician participation in executions; in general, they defer to the AMA. The issue of sanctioning or supporting a member who has participated or declined to participate in an execution

has yet to arise. They do not believe state law requires physician involvement.

SOUTH DAKOTA

Method of Execution: lethal injection. (Article 23A-27A-32 of *Criminal Procedure*, "Place and Manner of Execution;" Punishment is inflicted by lethal injection...)
State Statute Regarding Physicians' Role: Punishment is inflicted..."until the convict is pronounced dead by a licensed physician according to accepted standards of medical practice." The executioner must be trained to administer intravenous injections; the executioner "need not be a physician, registered nurse or licensed practical nurse." The procedure "may not be construed to be the practice of medicine..." Pharmacies can dispense drugs to the Warden without prescription. (Article 23A-27A-32 of *Criminal Procedure*, "Place and Manner of Execution.")
     "...the Warden shall also *arrange for* the attendance of the prison physician and two other licensed physicians of the state." (Article 23A-27A-34 of *Criminal Procedure*, "Persons Attending.")
Department of Corrections Regulations Regarding Physicians' Role: According to a letter from the Department of Corrections, South Dakota, whose most recent execution took place in 1947, does not have regulations for the administration of executions.
State Medical Society's Position: The South Dakota State Medical Association has no policy statement on physicians' role in executions.

TENNESSEE

Method of Execution: electrocution. (Article 40-23-144 of *Tennessee Code Annotated Volume* 7, "Death by electrocution.")
State Statute Regarding Physicians' Role: "Witnesses" includes the prison physician. (Article 40-23-116 of *Tennessee Code Annotated Volume* 7.)
Department of Corrections Regulations Regarding Physicians' Role:
In a July 30, 1992, letter, the Commissioner of the Tennessee Department of Corrections informed us that "In order to sustain the security and integrity of the institution, I regret that I am unable to send you more specific information regarding executions."
State Medical Society's Position: The Tennessee Medical Association does not have a policy regarding physician participation in executions. The

issue has yet to have been addressed and they are unaware of state law on the subject.

TEXAS

Method of Execution: lethal injection. (Article 43.14 of *Texas Criminal Laws*, "Execution of Convict;" punishment is inflicted by lethal injection.)
State Statute Regarding Physicians' Role: Those "Present at execution" includes two physicians, including the prison physician.
(Article 43.20 [804] of *Texas Criminal Laws.)*
Department of Corrections Regulations Regarding Physicians' Role: The "Texas Department of Corrections Procedures for the Execution of Inmates Sentenced to Death" states: "A medically trained individual (not to be identified) shall insert an intravenous catheter into the condemned person's arm and cause a neutral saline solution to flow." After the prisoner completes his/her last statement, the designee(s) of the Director "...shall induce by syringe substance and/or substances necessary to cause death. This individual(s) shall be visually separated from the execution chamber by a wall and locked door, and shall also not be identified." The attending physician(s) shall stand with the witnesses.
State Medical Society's Position: The Texas Medical Association has a policy statement opposing doctors' participation in executions.

UTAH

Method of Execution: firing squad or lethal injection. (Article 77-19-10 of *Utah Criminal Code*, "Judgement of death - location and procedures" (1), (2), and (3); The death warrant specifies the method of execution...)
State Statutes Regarding Physicians' Role: If judgement is to be carried out by shooting, the executive director selects a five-person firing squad of "peace officers." If the judgement is to be carried out by lethal injection, the executive director must select two or more persons "trained in accordance with accepted medical practices to administer intravenous injections..." Death shall be pronounced by a licensed physician "according to accepted medical standards."
(Article 77-19-10 of *Utah Criminal Code*, "Judgement of death - location and procedures" (2) and (3).)

The executive director "shall cause a physician to attend the execution." (Article 77-19-11 of *Utah Criminal Code*, "Who may be present...")

Department of Corrections Regulations Regarding Physicians' Role:
The Utah Department of Corrections declined to provide us with regulations detailing the execution process. At our request, the Assistant Director of the Department cited the Utah Code Annotated 63-2-304 (a) (11) as the basis for confidentiality.

State Medical Society's Position: The Utah Medical Association has a policy statement opposing doctors' participation in executions and procedures for disciplining doctors who participate in executions and to assist those who refuse.

VIRGINIA

Method of Execution: electrocution. (Article 53.1-233 of *Code of Virginia*, "Method;" punishment is inflicted by electrocution and is conducted by the Director or one or more of his designees.)

State Statutes Regarding Physicians' Role: Those present include the physician employed by the Department or his assistant. (Article 53.1-234 of *Code of Virginia*, "Who to be present.")

The physician shall perform an examination to determine that death has occurred; the physician's death certificate is appended to the Director's certification. (Article 53.1-235 of *Code of Virginia*, "Certificate of execution.")

Department of Corrections Regulations Regarding Physicians' Role:
The Deputy Director of Virginia Department of Corrections stated in a July 7, 1992 letter that "information which is related to security procedures or the release of which could jeopardize institutional security or client confidentiality will not be provided to your organization." On these grounds, the warden of Greensville Correctional Center, the institution where executions are carried out, declined to provide us with regulations regarding executions. He did state in his letter that the "attending physician pronounces the inmate deceased approximately five minutes upon the completion of the process."

State Medical Society's Position: The Medical Society of Virginia does not have a policy on physician participation in executions; they defer to the AMA. It is up to a committee to determine if a member has committed a breach of ethics; if so, there is the possibility the member will be expelled. The Society might support a member who declined to participate; there is no policy in place to do so at this time. They do not believe state law requires physician involvement, the current execution procedure being electrocution.

WASHINGTON

Method of Execution: lethal injection or hanging. (Amendment to Article 10.95.180 of *Criminal Procedure*.) The punishment of death shall be inflicted by intravenous injection of a substance or substances in a lethal quantity sufficient to cause death and until the defendant is dead, or at the election of the defendant, by hanging the neck until the defendant is dead.

State Statutes Regarding Physicians' Role: Punishment is...to be supervised by the superintendent of the state Penitentiary; "until death is pronounced by a licensed physician." (Article 10.95.180 of *Criminal Procedure*, Method; (1).)

Department of Corrections Regulations Regarding Physicians' Role: A physician is among the staff members required/permitted to attend the execution. The physician will determine if death has occurred. B. The physician and coroner will: 1. Make pronouncement of death. 2. Sign the death certificate.

Appendix B - DEATH BY LETHAL INJECTION states that as soon as the inmate has elected lethal intravenous injection, a physical examination will be conducted to determine any physical problems that may affect the execution process. A copy of this examination along with any recommendations will be forwarded immediately to the designated associate superintendent. (Department of Corrections Policy No. 01.100.)

State Medical Society's Position: The Washington State Medical Association's policy is that physician participation in a legally authorized execution be discouraged. They would sanction a member who acted in contravention of this policy, but such a situation has yet to arise. They would probably support a member who declined to participate. They do not believe state law requires physician involvement.

WYOMING

Method of Execution: lethal injection. (Article 7-13-904 of *Wyoming Statutes 1977*, "Method of execution;" Punishment is inflicted by lethal injection...)

State Statutes Regarding Physicians' Role: Punishment is inflicted...until death is pronounced by a licensed physician "according to accepted standards of medical practice." "Administration of the injection does not constitute the practice of medicine."

"Witnesses" include (ii) two (2) physicians, including the prison physician. (Article 7-13-908 of *Wyoming Statutes 1977.*)

Department of Corrections Regulations Regarding Physicians' Role: The Director of Wyoming Department of Corrections, in a June 15, 1992 letter stated that the departmental policies and procedures regarding executions are confidential and may not be publicly released. Our follow up request to cite the grounds for this confidentiality went unanswered.

State Medical Society's Position: The Wyoming Medical Society has no policy statement on physicians' role in executions because the Society defers on this issue to the position taken by the American Medical Association.